What Do You Want from Me?

ALSO BY TERRI APTER

*The Sister Knot: Why We Fight, Why We're Jealous, and Why We'll Love
  Each Other No Matter What*

*You Don't Really Know Me: Why Mothers and Daughters Fight and How Both
  Can Win*

The Myth of Maturity: What Teenagers Need from Parents to Become Adults

The Confident Child: Raising Children to Believe in Themselves

Secret Paths: Women in the New Midlife

Best Friends: The Perils and Pleasures of Girls' and Women's Friendships
  (with Ruthellen Josselson)

Altered Loves: Mothers and Daughters During Adolescence

Working Women Don't Have Wives: Professional Success in the 1990s

WHAT DO YOU WANT FROM ME?

Learning to Get Along with In-Laws

TERRI APTER

W. W. NORTON & COMPANY

New York · London

For information about permission to reproduce selections from this book,
write to Permissions, W. W. Norton & Company, Inc.,
500 Fifth Avenue, New York, NY 10110

For information about special discounts for bulk purchases, please contact
W. W. Norton Special Sales at specialsales@wwnorton.com or 800-233-4830

Manufacturing by RR Donnelley, Bloomsburg
Book design by Charlotte Staub
Production manager: Julia Druskin

Library of Congress Cataloging-in-Publication Data

Apter, T. E.
What do you want from me? : learning to get along with in-laws / Terri
Apter. — 1st ed.
    p. cm.
Includes bibliographical references and index.
ISBN 978-0-393-06697-5 (hardcover)
1. Parents-in-law. 2. Interpersonal relations. I. Title.
HQ759.8.A68 2009
646.7'8—dc22

                                        2009013159

ISBN 978-0-393-33853-9 pbk.

W. W. Norton & Company, Inc.
500 Fifth Avenue, New York, N.Y. 10110
www.wwnorton.com

W. W. Norton & Company Ltd.
Castle House, 75/76 Wells Street, London W1T 3QT

1 2 3 4 5 6 7 8 9 0

Contents

Acknowledgments

What Do You Want from Me? emerges from the rich stories provided by the people who have collaborated with me by being "subjects" of research. I ask a great deal of my interviewees: I ask them to reflect on difficult problems; I ask them to expose family tensions; and I ask them to tease out details of their own and others' behavior that, ordinarily, they would prefer to ignore. They made records of family gatherings, sometimes by writing diaries, sometimes by taping their own commentaries on fluctuating thoughts and feelings and observations during family holidays, weekend visits, and even, in one case, a wedding. To the 49 families and 156 people who participated in my research, I owe everything.

I am so lucky to have Jill Bialosky at W. W. Norton as an editor who responds to proposals with imaginative and critical sympathy. Meg Ruley and Kelly Harms at Jane Rotrossen Agency were outstanding champions of this project from the outset, and guided me with keen eyes and good humor through a series of proposals.

My colleagues at Newnham are always ready to engage with my ideas; they offer valuable ongoing conversations in which

I can test the resonance of themes that emerge in my research. Jenny Mander and Sheila Watts never let me let go of the subject of in-laws. Susan Golombok, Liba Taub, and Diana Lipton, with understated persistence, assured me that in-law relationships were worth further exploration. Their interest and encouragement kept this project in the forefront of my mind for many years.

Beverly and Alan Freid, with their Web site www.motherinlaw stories.com, brought my work on in-laws to a global audience; they also brought me stories of people desperate to make sense of these compelling, challenging relationships. Since 1999, they have shared their fascination in this subject with me.

Even a brief conversation with Carol Gilligan can reframe entrenched assumptions, and, as always, I am grateful for her creative, imaginative engagement with my ideas. Janet Reibstein offered me the benefit of her many years' experience as a marital therapist, and guided me through the structures of common interactions. Jeannette Josse generously set out a psychoanalytic template that explains common patterns of conflict.

A FINAL note about grammar: Following rules of grammar strictly sometimes leads to awkward-sounding phrases; in this book, I often follow my ear, rather than strict rules of grammar, in using the plural and possessive forms of "in-laws." Also, I sometimes use the plural "they" in cases that grammatically require the singular "he" or "she." And I sometimes use "she" or "he" to designate "any person" when the matter is more likely to involve women or men; this is not intended to exclude anyone of either gender from the full range of experiences. The words I use are chosen for ease and immediacy, and I hope my choices will be tolerated.

Introduction

WHEN I was first married, as a very young woman, I believed that I was embarking on a partnership between two people, and only two. As a typical twentieth-century woman, I imagined that once we called ourselves grown-ups, we snapped those child-hood bonds to parents, and slipped into adult life with neat, clean boundaries. I had no inkling of the range of influences or the pull of old bonds that would gradually be exposed—strong, stubborn, and exacting. Consequently, I lacked foresight of the power that would be wielded by a family who I initially supposed were mere add-ons to my husband. In short, I failed to measure the impact my in-laws would have on my marriage, my personal life, and my well-being.

At the same time, one of the many things I found so attractive in my husband was his capacity for love, loyalty, and attachment. I admired the spontaneous decency that bound him to his mother, his father, and his sister. Oblivious to my inconsistency, my view was skewed by self-interest. I saw his family ties as indicators of strong future attachments to his own wife and children, but without force in and of themselves. Not only did I assume that my parents-in-law would be marginal players in my own life, I expected that whatever impact they had would decrease further as we established ourselves as a couple, the primary group of our very own family. Growing up, I thought, meant that the older generation ceased to matter.

I never expected that my in-laws would shape as many of my day-to-day thoughts and moods as they in fact have, that they would color my sense of who I am and what I'm worth in the family, or that their needs would stake such a large claim on family decisions. In short, like many people embarking on marriage, I failed to gauge the inescapable power of in-laws.

Now, as a parent facing the transition to mother-in-law, I have a very different view, though this new perspective is perhaps equally skewed by self-interest. The bond I have with my children, whatever their age, however mature and independent they become, is forever, and, from my perspective, will not diminish when they marry. My own children's interests will continue to take priority on any and every scale, and I will measure their partners according to their value and benefit to my own children. I will try to follow reasonable rules about privacy and boundaries, but my maternal heart will not be modified by common sense or wise precept. My research on in-laws suggests that my "double-think" places me in the majority.

The topic of in-laws is a lightning rod, charged with confusion and fear. That is one reason why jokes about in-laws are so common. Sometimes we laugh when we are anxious and bewildered. Through laughter, we can temporarily release tension and share our discomfort, but jokes do not provide the insight we need to manage these relationships. What is needed is deep understanding of the many levels on which the power of in-laws is enacted.

The in-laws we acquire when we marry are embedded in the lives of people we love. They see themselves as the source of a child's life; they crave assurance of continuing family bonds; they monitor a child's happiness, at every stage of life. They have a passionate interest in their children's children. In turn, their children respond powerfully to them, at every stage of life. In-laws come glued to the people we choose as partners. It is high time that the impact of in-laws is acknowledged and understood.

Much of the power of in-laws arises from positive sources. Families map out a paradigm of human connection. They are the most effective social structure known for promoting people's health and well-being throughout their lives. But families also provide a setting for day-to-day emotional drama that ranges from superficial and transient discomfort to profound and lasting pain. Much has been written about the deep and abiding problems that arise when families function poorly, but little has been written about the complex gamut from happiness to despair that arises within the overlapping families formed by marriage.

During the past two decades, my research has dealt with many family relationships—mothers and teenagers, siblings, and parents and their young adult children. But the always complex and often uncomfortable relationships between in-laws have also been a long-term interest of mine.

In primary relationships, I observe a struggle to get things right, to preserve love, and to provide protection. In other words, goodwill is paramount. In interviews and observations of overlapping families, however, I come face-to-face with uncomfortable truths about tension and jealousy. In the context of in-laws, many people have a tendency towards bias and resentment that does not emerge in their behavior elsewhere, with a partner, blood family,[1] or friends.

Second, I have discovered that such behavior often leads to long-term distress, and to the severe deterioration of a marriage.

Third, I have observed how in-law conflict is embedded within kinship structures and family systems. It is never simple, and seldom arises simply between two people.

Fourth, I have listened as people pleaded for help in understanding these relationships and in devising strategies to resolve in-law conflict, and complained that there were few resources to guide them.

Listening to people talk about their lives is gripping, but the interviews I conducted were also intensive and exhausting. Talking to people about their in-laws can be a strange and perplexing experience. As people speak, they seem to grasp at something they cannot fully make sense of. A frenzy of anger is followed by a spasm of self-doubt: "Who is at fault?" and "Am I justified in feeling insulted/slighted/imposed upon/criticized?" Anger shifts from one in-law to the other, then to a partner, and back again. In the presence of your in-laws, your worst side emerges—a less tolerant, less open, less fun, less kind persona than is consistent with the person you think you really are.

While many people are willing to talk informally and sporadically about their family and the in-laws who play a significant role in the wide context of family dynamics, the people who participated in my studies showed an extraordinary willingness to engage with difficult, uncomfortable questions. They grappled with their guilt and ambivalence, and in so doing they

helped me discover where the fracture lines lay. With their help,
I discovered which of the many combinations of in-law relationships are the most difficult, and why difficulties arise, how they
affect marriage, and how they might be resolved. I interviewed
people individually and with their partners; I observed family
gatherings; I read the diaries and records my collaborators kept
at my request. Perhaps it is the hunger for understanding and
resolution that stimulated the generous and brave responses of
my interviewees.

A hundred and fifty volunteers responded to invitations I
made to audiences and organizers of my public lectures. In the
end, I was able to complete interviews with 49 couples and their
in-laws.[2] Thirty-two were in the United States and 17 were from
the United Kingdom. The couples ranged in age from twenty-
two to fifty-four, and the age of parents-in-law spanned from
forty-three to eighty. The 156 primary participants included 52
Caucasians, 33 from the United States and 19 from Britain; 32
African Americans; 24 Hispanic Americans; 25 Asian Americans; and 23 Asian British.

The interviews are rich and varied, and they offer many possible interpretations. Interview subjects revise and process their
stories in accord with their own feelings and needs. A challenge
in interpreting such material is to avoid both naïveté and cyni-
cism. The meanings people attach to others' behavior have to
be respected. At the same time, other possible perspectives have
to be imagined, and different views of different people have to
fit into the picture.

The interpretative approach I take has some similarities to
critical readings of a text. I read and reread the material. I note
recurring themes. I try out theories of explanation, which I then

revise or discard or develop. I stick with and refine the theories that resonate with and make sense of the material as a whole. In this way, I follow the most rigorous methods possible for uncovering the realities of these conundrums.[3]

Among those I interviewed were people who loved their parents-in-law and people who loved their children-in-law, sometimes even more than their blood relatives. Some saw their in-laws as exciting and rewarding additions to their lives. But among those who suffered from in-law conflict, distinctive, claustrophobic patterns emerged. People who have primarily positive relationships with their in-laws are skeptical as to the genuine causes of in-law conflict and the significance of the difficulties that arise. Those who experience these problems, on the other hand, engage in emotionally draining mental maneuvers to defend themselves, to make sense of their anger, and to find strategies for controlling the whirlwind of emotions that hits them when their in-laws enter their homes. They try to preserve their sanity, without destroying other family bonds. All too often, they struggle in isolation. My research pools experiences of many families and shows effective strategies for resolving anger, humiliation, and despair.

"What do you want from me?" is such a common cri de coeur when in-law relationships go wrong that it became the title of this book. "What do you want from me?" marks the outrage at demands and criticisms that seem out of step with everything you have previously experienced in your interpersonal world.

Many of the chapters take their titles from other questions that became familiar during the course of the interviews. "Why Does It Go Wrong?" looks at the primary sources of conflict. "Are You

Really Part of My Family?" looks at the ways a family may either mark itself as the dominant family or ensure that a new member conforms to the family's rules. In Chapter Four, "Why Is It So Hard on the Women?" I explain why broad-based in-law conflicts tend to be enacted by the women in the family, and why women tend to suffer most—or most obviously—from in-law conflict. Chapter Five, "Whose Side Are You On?" describes the struggles for a partner's support, and the dilemmas of love and loyalty that arise where in-law conflict is concerned. The next chapter, "What Is Happening To Me?" traces the transition to mother-in-law, and describes experiences that have largely been hidden by negative stereotypes. Chapter Seven, "Is Any of This My Fault?" asks hard questions about our own biases and our own tendencies to discount others' criticism. It explores how we shape memories to bolster our egos, sometimes unfairly. This may be the book's most challenging chapter, for I ask readers to consider how they themselves may be contributing to their problems with in-laws. Chapter Eight, "Who's the Mother Now?" traces another transition as the parents-in-law become grandparents. In Chapter Nine, "What Do I Owe You?" I consider the tricky obligations and resentments that arise when there are financial exchanges between families. Next, in "Who Do You Think You Are?" I concentrate on lateral in-law relationships—sister-in-law and brother-in-law. While these share many aspects of cross-generational in-law relationships, such as loyalty, protectiveness, and competition, their links to sibling alliances, power play, and hostilities require a chapter of their own. In Chapter Eleven, "Are We Still Family?" I show the surprising strength of these bonds beyond marriage. In the final chapter, "Getting Along and Looking Forward," I consider how the power of these bonds is expressed through care and continuity.

What Do You Want from Me? explains why in-laws have power; it outlines the common ways this power is exercised; and it shows how we can grasp that power to secure our well-being within family networks. It draws on three studies I have conducted over the past fifteen years, and it also draws on follow-up and feedback responses from the public. At a meeting of the British Psychological Association, I presented research that pinpoints the most difficult in-law tension as that between mother-in-law and daughter-in-law. This academic paper aroused a storm of media interest.[4] In the wake of this, Beverly and Alan Freid invited me to contribute to their Web site motherinlawstories .com. Since 2000 I have received over a thousand stories, questions, and pleas for help from people throughout the United States and the United Kingdom who feel isolated, infuriated, and confused by the difficulties that arise from these bonds.

Some books on in-laws propose categories of difficult in-laws: those who meddle, those who control, those who criticize, those who bully or blackmail. But in-law relationships are difficult because in-laws do not sit firmly in any category. We can see that they are difficult sometimes but also helpful at others, that they sometimes bully us but are sometimes supportive.

In all close relationships, we have to accept a mix of qualities. In all close relationships, we have to accept our own mixed feelings. We begin this acceptance in infancy when we integrate our love for our parents with our rage against our parents when they are not perfectly responsive to us and lack the power to protect us from all human ills. We continue this emotional integration with our siblings, whom we love and whom we also fear and resent as rivals. We make a pledge to continue integrating positive and negative feelings when we promise to take the rough and the smooth in marriage. When it comes to in-laws, we may lack the strong emotional bond that facilitates integration of mixed feelings with other family members. Nonetheless, we can learn how to manage these relationships, to improve them, and to foster what is good in them.

What Do You Want from Me?

1.

The Inescapable Power of In-Laws

WHEN two people marry, they form a family of their own, brand new and full of promise. While the couple focus on each other and their own future, they also join another family with whom they will interact, intimately and passionately. Even brief exchanges with in-laws can raise powerful feelings, yet few people enter marriage prepared to manage the impact their new overlapping family has on them, their marriage, their day-to-day actions, and their lifelong obligations.

The Structural Power of In-Laws

Couples are often stunned by the impact of their overlapping family. They may be blinded to the importance of overlapping families by the myth that families are "nuclear." The reality and persistence of the extended family is one of the best-kept secrets of modern times; yet extended families form a fundamental building block for the well-being of all family members.[1]

Commentators endlessly discuss the decline of the family, citing the decrease in marriage, the increase of divorces and separations, and the high number of single parents as signs of over-

all family decline.[2] By some measures, the "horizontal" family
declined in stability from 1950 until about 2004[3]; but divorce
rates constitute only one measure of family life.[4] The "vertical"
family is routinely overlooked in assessments of the strength of
family bonds. The bonds between parent and child and grandchild have not weakened. The blood family endures as a key
social and emotional structure. In consequence, parents remain
passionately concerned about the quality and nature of a child's
marriage, and therefore have a vested interest in a son-in-law or
daughter-in-law. As grandparents, they feel intimately involved
with the quality of their grandchildren's care, and have a vital
concern about their son-in-law's or daughter-in-law's parenting.
Whether our in-laws are frequent visitors, or whether we rarely
set eyes on them, they remain part of our family.

The power of in-laws speaks to the strength of family connection. It challenges the myth that in maturity we separate
from parents. With the lengthy and complex transition from
youth to adulthood, parents continue to play an important part
in their daughters' and sons' lives, well beyond the first decade
of adulthood. These enduring attachments between parents
and their children and their children's children support young
adults' long odyssey from youth to maturity.

Being "independent"—becoming what we think of as a real
grown-up—does not mean we sever these emotional bonds
with parents. Grown men and women maintain a high level
of attachment to their parents. They continue to be pleased
by parental approval and piqued by parental criticism. Above
all, they expect that they will remain of key interest to their
parents.

The pulls of loyalty and love between parent and child are

lifelong. Grown-ups need to check in with a parent, just as they did as kids. In midlife, they often want to reciprocate and offer care to an infirm or a lonely elderly parent who provided for them in their youth. Studies show, repeatedly, that the well-being of women and men in midlife is enhanced by good quality relationships with their own parents.[5] When parents age, sons and daughters usually step up to provide help, at great cost to themselves. The impact—practical, emotional, and financial—of such care on families has increased in recent decades as the life span of their parents increases. It is a myth that adult children, or their partners, abandon elderly parents.[6]

Attachments to parents run deep and, whether for good or ill, impact all other intimate connections. Grandparents offer practical, financial, and emotional help in raising grandchildren. Parents continue to offer support as their adult children juggle the demands of work and family. Adult children, in turn, feel responsible for the well-being of their parents. Such bonds remain of the utmost social and emotional importance.

Cross-generational ties have in many ways strengthened during the past two generations. While baby boomers—people born between 1945 and 1960—were expected to stand on their own two feet financially and emotionally as soon as they reached the age of adulthood, subsequent generations confront a range of social and financial pressures that make such independence an unhealthy, unrealistic ideal.[7] And while couples often need financial and practical support from their parents, their longer-living parents are likely to experience illness and infirmity that call up strong responses and support from adult children. A new phase of family connection emerges as midlife people continue to demonstrate love and care to elderly parents. Bonds to parents impact our partners, and the long, complex story of in-law relationships is told by people of all ages.

A Couple's Needs

A primary need in marriage is for mutuality and support. We expect to be the most important person in our partner's life. Phrases such as "You're *the* one" and "You come first" mark some of the many ways this norm is endorsed.

The expectation of perfect mutuality and support takes many different shapes. It may come as an expectation that your partner will respect or even venerate your parents. It may come as an expectation that your partner will protect you from difficult parents. Whether or not these expectations are voiced, each person in a couple needs the other as an ally in the challenges and burdens and pleasures of fulfilling family duties. We may, with the inconsistency of bias, both expect a partner to accommodate our blood family *and* expect that we will never have to modify our needs on behalf of our own new family of in-laws. The loyalty pulls of different families may cause confusion and outrage. In this way, family bonds can tear a family apart.

The Psychological Power of In-Laws

As we join a new family, many of the hopes, fears, and needs that arise from our experiences within our primary family are re-awakened. Though these hopes, fears, and needs sometimes function beneath our conscious radar, they shape our interactions with in-laws. In fact, the starting position for both hope and disappointment is the fantasy that our overlapping family will provide us with new, improved versions of our primary family.

A daughter-in-law expects that her husband's parents will be thrilled to welcome her into their family and will appreciate what she brings to their son's life. A mother-in-law expects that someone who loves her son will respect and admire her maternal input. A father-in-law expects that his position in the family will be respected. A son-in-law hopes for respect, support, and admiration for all that he can offer his wife and children.

Sometimes these expectations are met. Sometimes they are cruelly disappointed. The dark side of in-laws, with its fairy-tale menace, emerges when these unacknowledged expectations are disappointed. When we are not embraced as the new, perfect daughter, or appreciated as the ideal mother, this disappointment colors our view of the person who disappoints us. Thus, disappointment gives these relationships their distinctive negative charge.

Then, there is the fear that a son's or daughter's romantic attachment will shatter the bond to a parent. "What will I have to relinquish (in terms of closeness and influence) to make room for someone else in the family?" is a question that may haunt us as we see our child make a commitment to form a new family.

Parents-in-law normally acknowledge the general rule that a couple's privacy has to be respected. At the same time, there are follow-on concerns: "What is the new boundary between me and my married child?" and "How will this affect my own precious relationship to my child?"

The process of becoming a couple will change each partner's relationship with their own parents. One partner might have an internal, perhaps unspoken model of marriage as purely private and self-contained. The other partner might hold a more inclusive, clannish family model, with marriage as a network of kinship. For a parent-in-law, the paramount question is: "Does my child's partner see the marriage as including me, or excluding me?"

Parents share an interest in how marriage will change their relationship with a son or daughter. Common sense might lead us to conclude that the altruistic pull of parental love inspires us to love those who play important and positive roles in a son's or daughter's life; but there is also a more selfish side to parental love that we cannot ignore if we want to understand the power of in-laws. While a parent's love is often seen as the best model of truly altruistic behavior, there are good evolutionary reasons why parents have a very selfish-seeming need to retain a close bond with their children. Parents may be willing to give up everything—even their lives—for their children's survival, but embedded in their psychology is a need to retain a connection to their children. The marriage of a daughter or son involves a transition in which some loss, or fear of loss, has to be negotiated. Any parent is likely to feel uneasy about what she might have to relinquish. Parents need to see their children thrive as independent adults, *and* they need to maintain an enduring connection to their children.

The Cultural Power of In-Laws

To feel comfortable in a family, we must be able to express our thoughts and feelings, and to engage in those uniquely human exchanges that constitute domestic intimacy. Quite simply, we expect to feel "at home" among our family, with the fluency of communication this implies. Each family forms an intensely emotional system in which its members learn how to develop and regulate close human relationships. In our primary families we learn to anticipate how others will respond to what we say and what we do, and we learn what return we might expect from our own love acts, as well as what punishments we might expect from our acts of defiance.

We also learn strategies for making amends, so we can repair good relationships when anger erupts. In these lessons, we acquire our own quirky measure of what counts as normal. Often we come to believe that what we learn about the norms of our own individual family is universal. When we join an over-lapping family, however, we tend to have a rude awakening.

Two people from different families may communicate easily and, together, establish their own set of interpersonal norms. But beyond the boundaries of their private love will be the interper-sonal rules and emotional language they learned in their own families. These are never forgotten, replaced, or retired. When we follow our own family's rules in an overlapping family, we can find ourselves out of place—and nearly out of our minds.

The Hierarchical Power of In-Laws

When the interests and needs of overlapping families conflict, the members have to negotiate with one another and priori-tize different claims. In some cultures, one family—usually the husband's—takes precedence over the other. Its customs, aims, and needs dominate the new couple, and the young wife is then subservient to all her in-laws. This structural power was rarely exercised in the families participating in my studies, but power struggles between families remained an issue. Questions such as "Whose needs come first?" and "Whose unhappiness matters more?" spark conflict between a couple, between their siblings, and between their parents. Since your own family is likely to matter more to you than your in-laws, failure to negotiate priorities leads both to in-law conflict and marital conflict.

Mutuality means that each person's feelings and views carry weight. Being denied mutuality by our overlapping family makes us feel discounted and disrespected; such lack of mutuality, within the intimate family setting, arouses either fury or despair.[8] Having one's needs undercut, having one's thoughts undermined, and being positioned as a marginal member of a group drives a stake through the heart of family connections. "Whose family comes first?" is a question that can split a marriage in two.

The dynamics of in-law relationships are shaped by family structure, individual psychology, family culture, and hierarchy.

The Slow Dawning of the Significance of In-Laws

The power of in-laws has no official recognition at this time, in either of the countries from which my case studies are drawn. In-law tensions in the United States and the United Kingdom tend either to be shrugged off or surreptitiously shared in low-grade gossip. In-laws, and the conflicts that arise, are seen as among the uncomfortable but inevitable comedies of family life.

The most common way of managing in-law problems is through humor. A permission slip is provided for ruthless, tasteless, misogynist jibes when it comes to dealing with in-law problems. But this staple of the stand-up comedian's act fails to elucidate the highly charged and utterly confusing tensions between in-laws. The typical jokes are in a male voice: They are directed towards a mother-in-law by a son-in-law. Yet the crux of the problem is between women. Our failure to manage these powerful bonds puts at risk our marriage, our day-to-day comfort, and our long-term happiness.

In one European country, the potential force of in-laws on the viability of marriage is well researched; the findings have shaped policy, and legislation has been passed to defend the boundaries between in-laws and a married couple. When the Italian National Statistics Institute correlated divorce rates and living arrangements, it was found that the chances of a lasting marriage go up with every hundred yards that couples can put between themselves and their in-laws.[9] The responsibility of sustaining a suitable emotional distance is now put on the husband: Italy's highest court of appeal has ruled that a woman has the right to demand separation from her husband if he fails to prevent his mother from "invading" the marital home.

In the United States, more than 51 percent of the adult population is married and living with a spouse. This means that approximately 120 million people in the United States are likely to have in-laws at the present moment. The mean duration of marriage is twenty years, so any unresolved problems that arise with in-laws will have a long run. In the United States approximately 2.4 million couples marry each year.[10] The vast majority of newly married couples have parents who are alive and actively involved in their lives. This means that there are upwards of 9.6 million new in-law relationships created every year, and 75 percent of couples report that they have some problems with an in-law.[11]

In-law relationships and in-law problems also extend on either side of a marriage. Engaged couples tend to have significant interaction with a fiancé's family. The increasing number of people who form couples without being married (5.3 million couples) also are embedded in overlapping families. Those whose marriages end in death or in divorce, which affects 20.4 million people, have to engage and disengage with in-laws. In any couple, two people become members of a new family group. This new group includes the couple, one's own family of origin, and one's partner's family of origin. There are, it has been argued, six people in a marriage bed.[12]

Basic Steps to Comfortable In-Law Relationships

Managing relationships with in-laws involves a number of high-level skills. One must be able to understand problems, identify desirable changes, and form feasible strategies for dealing with the problems at hand.

The first step to forming a strategy is to grasp the complexity of even apparently simple conflicts. The key fact is that in-law problems are never simple and never involve simply two people.

The second step is to identify a possible outcome. What do you want to change?

Then you can come up with a feasible strategy to achieve that outcome. This will probably involve many changes—to your behavior, and to your partner's behavior, and only then will an in-law's behavior be modified. This is more of a challenge than managing your own behavior and moods. This involves painstaking work towards changing systems of interaction and "teaching" others to have different incentives. If they fear loss, then we need to find ways to reassure them; if they seek reassurance and control in ways that make us miserable, then we have to regularly disappoint them so that they will have incentives for changing their behavior.

The basic skills of in-law management are transferable skills. This means that they are skills that a person can acquire in many different contexts, and they are skills that can be used in a range of situations. Seeing how our own behavior should change is the greatest challenge in resolving in-law problems. When we are angry, when we feel disempowered or marginalized, it is difficult to demand of ourselves: "What role am I playing in maintaining this awful situation?" But we need to ask and answer this question if we are to grasp the complexity of a conflict, identify a reasonable outcome, and follow a strategy to achieve this. Then we can harness the power of in-laws to promote our and our family's well-being.

OVERVIEW

When we marry, we become part of a new extended family. We are likely to harbor expectations

- that the overlapping family will greet us as the perfect child/parent
- that our partner will offer us perfect support in everything
- that we share with our partner the same view of boundaries between us and our overlapping families
- that the interpersonal styles we learned in our primary family will work in our overlapping family

We may find that
- disappointed expectations lead to conflict
- conflict with in-laws spreads to marital conflict
- how we manage this conflict affects our long-term well-being

Learning how to manage this power is difficult. It is difficult because
- this power is unexpected
- the ways in-laws exercise power are varied and subtle
- the negative, hurtful messages and controls are usually mixed with positive messages of love and care
- the target of our anger shifts, so that we often do not know whom we are angry with
- we are often unsure of the legitimacy of our own complaints
- we tend to overlook the role we play in the situations that distress us
- in the heat of conflict, we overestimate others' power and underestimate our own

This book is a guide through the frustration, fear, and self-doubt generated by in-law conflict. It explains why we are so puzzled and exasperated by it, and assures us that the angry, rhetorical question "What do you want from me?" can be transformed into a guide through the maze of love and loyalty configured when families overlap.

2. Why Does It Go Wrong?
The Primary Source of Conflict

MARRIAGE is rich with the promise of enduring connection, personal happiness, and continuing family. But marriage is also hedged with uncertainties. Everyone with any affection for either person in the couple puts hope on full blast as they celebrate a marriage. Everyone related to the couple roots for their happiness. No one in either family starts out with the intention of adding to the couple's ordinary lot of difficulties. Yet three out of four couples experience significant conflict with their in-laws. Where does it all go wrong?

The people who love us usually provide crucial support in our marriage. In reflecting on his own ignorance at the time of his first marriage, Michael Chabon acknowledges that he did not have the faintest idea of the seriousness of this enterprise, or its challenges, or the reverberations that would follow its breakdown; but gradually he came to understand the meaning it had for his parents-in-law. Generally, when we marry, Chabon remarks, "We have no inkling of the fervor of their hope, nor of the ways in which our marriage, that collective endeavor, will be constructed from, and burdened by that love."[1]

The "collective endeavor" that both constructs and burdens

a marriage begins with parents' love for their own child. To gain some understanding of this collective endeavor, we have to consider the first passionate human bond, as consuming as any romance. And that is where in-law problems begin.

First Love

Human love has profound complexities and endless variations, but common patterns of mutual need for contact, continuity, and reassurance emerge in virtually all loving relationships. Each new person is born into the world actively prepared for emotional connections to other people. Helpless, save for a power to elicit love and responsiveness in others, the human infant is intensely sensitive to human faces, voices, and touch. The first people to welcome an infant into the world are usually the parents, and the parents are biologically, psychologically, and culturally prepared to be warm and engaged.

A passionate and absorbing bond with a parent is the infant's first experience of loving, and of being one person of a loving pair. Though romantic relationships are often understood to be very different from "blood" relationships, the chemistry of romantic love uses many of the same evolutionary strategies that bond mother to baby.

The biochemistry and neural signals that bond infant and parent are the very same ones, reused, in sexual attraction.[2] The parent/infant pair also act like lovers. A mother and baby lock together in a mutual gaze, each looking back to the other looking at her. This activity, practiced also by romantic lovers as they gaze at each other in mutual admiration, is called "eye love." The mother/infant couple engages, too, in an interpersonal dance of recognition in which each expresses exquisite responsiveness to every gesture and sound of the other. This primitive mutuality is called "I-to-I" engagement. It signals that intense focus on the other, shared by lovers.

For mother and infant, this early intimacy leaves a legacy that impacts on every subsequent passionate attachment. The aim of marriage, in many people's eyes, is to establish another intensely personal and exclusive bond. This of course does not replicate the parent/infant bond, but that first intimacy is a model of all love.

One of the important things people do as they establish themselves as a couple is negotiate and tame earlier romances. Many couples engage in complicated tactics to define past alliances as less important than this current, all-consuming one. Sharing past stories is a way of satisfying the hunger each has to know and understand the other, but these stories are also a means of diffusing the power of previous relationships. By sharing romantic histories, the previous experiences of each become joint emotional property. This joint ownership, hopefully, diffuses jealousy.

Past romances are not the only potentially competing bonds. The continuing love for parents, respect for family customs and values, and fear of parental disapproval and rejection stay with us long after we have pledged ourselves exclusively to a partner. The intensity and breadth of the parent/child bond may be neglected or ignored at the time of a couple's marriage, but it will remain active throughout their lives.

Mothers and Sons

Statements such as "She refuses to share her son" or "She doesn't want to let her son go" or "She cannot accept her son is grown up" fly frequently off the tongues of daughters-in-law. But is there a general refusal of a mother to "let go"? When the parent/infant passion is enacted by a mother and son, does it set up a competition between loving parent and lover? Do mothers really want their sons to themselves?[3]

These questions receive an emphatic "yes" from one third (sixteen) of the daughters-in-law I interviewed. In addition, over a quarter (thirteen) of daughters-in-law considered a partner's bond to a parent as driven by a *parent's* needs and demands. But a close look at their stories reveals a more complicated interpersonal dynamic than jealous maternal love.

If we are to understand in-law conflict, we may have to ignore everything we thought we knew about mothers and sons. Certainly, we have to unlearn every stereotype that marks our expectations. Conflict rarely arises from just one person's needs or one person's greed. Instead, several people respond to one another. These responses are shaped as much by long-standing fears and fantasies as they are by current situations. These responses generate their own demands and strategies, and these strategies are not always effective. In-laws are often caught in a system of interaction in which each person's responses reinforce the conflict they believe they are trying to resolve. The perspective of each is distorted by profound needs for love and recognition, and by overwhelming empathy with a parent's and partner's conflicting needs.

The most common pattern of conflict is enacted by a mother-in-law, a daughter-in-law, and the man who is both son and husband. It arises, generally, from a woman's anxiety, as mother, about change and consequent loss, and her anxiety, as mother-in-law, as to whether her role as mother will be appreciated, respected, and maintained. It arises equally from another woman's expectation that, as wife, she will be the most important woman in her husband's life, and, as daughter-in-law, she will be embraced, supported, and left alone, all at the same time. It arises, in equal measure, from a man's bemusement as to how to maintain and differentiate—or twin-track—two significant relationships, one as son and one as husband.

In her autobiographical piece about a silent but ferocious battle with her mother-in-law, Ayelet Waldman identifies a "tug-of-war between a mother and her daughter-in-law over a man [as] an age-old phenomenon, the stuff of sit-com jokes and Greek tragedy. Two women, decades apart, vying over the favors of a man who most often doesn't even know a battle is being fought."[4] This blueprint needs to be redrawn.

Key Questions as Guidance

While in-law problems have many permutations, a good starting point for the exploration of their strong and disturbing nature is in the mother/son bond. Gender shapes all relationships. A woman's experience of being loved and desired by a son has reverberations of romance in a way that a mother/daughter bond, though equally passionate, does not. This romantic echo in mother/son love increases the anxiety about what one will have to relinquish when her son marries. A key to understanding in-law conflict is to trace the vulnerability to its source. The guiding questions are,

"Who might experience a relational loss?"

"Whose status or power is in question?"

"Whose loved one is in need of protection?"

A parent-in-law who fears the loss of a treasured relationship, and who is unsettled by shifts in status and power, may allay her fears with "I'll prove that I'm the most important one in his life" and "I still have more influence on him than anyone else" and "I'm the one who knows him best and knows what he needs." These are strategies for managing vulnerability.

These strategies come in three broad guises: making demands, being intrusive, and sulking or eliciting pity. These strategies lock in-laws into a competition, thereby making all three people lose. These strategies screen the emotions that underpin them, and they generate the stereotypes that increase discomfort and unfairness between in-laws. Each person could win if the relationships became collaborative, if each, instead of confronting the other, would celebrate and reassure the other. The following case studies show how difficult this is to do, yet how easily it could be achieved.

Melissa, Jon, and Ashley:
Loss Managed by Demands

Melissa, who has been married to Jon for six years, explained that she and her mother-in-law, Ashley, got on well, initially.

When I was just Jon's girlfriend, things were fine. Nothing like the stickiness, the downright rage I feel now. I didn't visit Ashley a lot but when I did she seemed pleased to see me, and we talked about all sorts of things. Then, in that far-off pre-engagement era, we seemed to have enough in common to have a conversation.

It's amazing how different things were then. It's like she was a different person. When I knew her then, you know, before Jon and I were a real couple, she seemed very independent. She'd been divorced for a decade, and she'd retired, even when I first met her, but she seemed to have her own life, her own set of friends, and knew how to deal with those little things that life's always throwing at you, like a leaking water heater or a bad cold. She didn't strike me as someone who needs to be taken care of.

I knew Jon would visit her without me sometimes, and help her with this and that, but it wasn't a big thing, and it always seemed that it was his idea. He seemed to have this little tick on a mental calendar. "I should visit my mom this weekend," he'd say, and that was fine, because we could plan for it, and I'd just set up other things to do. It's really—you know, it's odd going back to how I once saw her. Because I thought she was one of those people who's really comfortable with herself. Maybe she was kind of reserved, but not in a way that made me uneasy. But when Jon told her were getting married—and I mean the *day* he told her—something changed. Like suddenly there was something going on I couldn't fathom. But I thought, give it time. Give her time. You know, here I am, such a nice person. What woman wouldn't be delighted to have me as a daughter-in-law? Ha! I don't say that now. There are all these lumpy issues, and they just keep getting thicker.

When I ask Melissa whether there is one "lumpy issue" that causes her particular distress, she says, without hesitation, that her primary complaint is about Ashley's demands on Jon. Melissa and Jon live in Chicago, and Ashley lives in Springfield, which Melissa describes as "a hard three and a half hours' drive, if you're lucky." Jon is a software consultant with a portfolio of jobs. Melissa is an accountant, and works more regular hours than Jon, but still often finds she has to work evenings "otherwise the next day is hell because things just pile up." A great enjoyment in being a couple, she explains, is "having downtime together, just hanging out, and then being free to do something together. That's mostly a weekend thing, very precious. And now we have this cute little house that needs stuff done to it, and it's nice to do it together. That feeling—this house is ours and our life is going to be lived here, and working on the house is kind of working on our future, making it how we want it— well, it gives me a deep, cozy feeling." Melissa feels that Ashley is depriving her of this simple comfort.

> She thinks it's perfectly okay to ask Jon to work in her yard on a weekend, or to fix a window that sticks, and leave me alone. I tell Jon I really want him here, and he gets impatient and tells me he'll do stuff here, too, when he gets back. But that's not the point. I just don't want him at her beck and call.

Melissa has tried what she calls "the direct approach":

> My heart was hammering so loud I thought everyone could hear it. I was so dreading any confrontation. But I was too fired up to back down. I explained that we'd have to space our visits, and that it wasn't fair to Jon to ask him to come

so often. He was missing out on clients. We were missing out on time we needed together. She seemed to catch on immediately. She raised herself up, wide-eyed and innocent: "I wouldn't dream of imposing on you," and "Of course, I want him to relax when he's home."

This took me by surprise, and I was thinking, "Gosh that was easy," and "Why didn't I say something before?" But then, surprise, surprise, nothing changed! "That's your *mom* on the phone?" I asked him. "You're going to your *mom's* on Saturday?" He was sheepish, and annoyed. You know: why was I surprised? What was the big deal? Well, it was a big deal, and I was furious with her. So we—I mean Jon and I—had a terrible fight when I said he was always going to his mother's. He was at her beck and call. And he said that was hogwash, he hardly ever went to see her.

Melissa's story seems clear-cut: her mother-in-law is too possessive. The solution seems simple: Ashley should accept that her son is his own man with his own marriage.

But every in-law story has many versions. As we trace the vulnerability—as we consider, "Who has an important relationship at risk?" and "Whose status is under threat?"—we are likely to find that more than one person is generating a conflict. Melissa, like Ashley, is vulnerable: Her special relationship with her husband is at risk, and her status in the family is called into question, and she, too, has strategies for addressing her vulnerability. But we catch sight of this only when we hear her mother-in-law's story.

Ashley's Story

Ashley is cautious as she describes her experience of her daughter-in-law. She confirms that her response to Melissa changed when she heard Jon planned to marry her.

Before, she was just another girlfriend, and I didn't feel anything in particular. Jon had a lot of girlfriends. He's very attractive, and, well, my worry was that he was so handsome he'd be a real heart-breaker. But I stopped worrying about that. His girlfriends probably gave as good as they got, you know? Not all of them wanted to settle down. They weren't always so nice, either. But I got used to them, and there were four or so over the years he brought home. Melissa was just another one.

He told me, real low key: "Mom, Mel and I have decided to get married." He seemed to want to drop it in softly, no noise, no fuss. So I just nodded. But it really hit me: why her? What was so special about her? So I asked if he was sure, and he said he was, and then I thought I'd better keep my mouth shut. There's something cold about her, cold and uncaring. She has ways of telling me, sort of sideways, that she doesn't like me. But that's not it. The thing is, she doesn't have any use for me. Every personal thing I say to Jon makes her freeze, and she throws a fit every time I ask Jon to do something, no matter how little. So, I have to admit, there are still times I look at her and think, "Why her?" And I get the creeps, and have to turn away, because if I look at her for too long, I get an urge to hit her.

The Myth of the Jealous Mother

Like many myths, the myth of the jealous and possessive mother is in some ways true and in some ways false. Distinguishing truth from falsehood, and recognizing the truth within falsehood, are key to understanding the conflict between mother-in-law and daughter-in-law.

Mother/child love changes, and both mother and child have to negotiate apparent losses as they move on. The baby, for example, may lose his status as "the only one" when a sibling is born, but he gains a companion and champion, as well as a competitor. The physical intimacy between his parents seems to exclude him, but also bonds his parents, strengthening his crucial support system.

These *necessary losses* are a part of life.[5] The realization that a mother's love can never be ours alone and that the people we love will age and die terrifies a dependent child; but accepting the need to share, to respect boundaries and privacy, and to accommodate change have the huge benefit of allowing us to extend our network of human connection. Over time, a parent also confronts the necessary loss of a child's intense dependence and the child's focus on a parent as "the one." Some parents have a pang of regret at each developmental milestone—for example, when a child leaves the house for his first day at school, shows romantic interest in a friend for the first time, or leaves home for college or a real grown-up job. A parent may feel momentarily sad at the "loss" of a child's dependence, but such "losses" are also sources of delight and pride.

There are many resources for advice and support for parents as their children undergo significant changes—from single child to sibling, as they start school, or as they leave home as young adults. But there is little available to advise and support parents in the transition from parent to parent-in-law. This is a significant and notoriously difficult transition that signals a definitive shift in emotional and psychological alliance, but parents are left alone to negotiate a transition foisted upon them by someone else's decision to marry.

A son's commitment to being a husband shifts his primary attachment from parent to spouse. As with any developmental step, the pleasure and promise of seeing an adult son or daughter form a new family means having to relinquish something—something not quite defined, with unknown ramifications. However pleased parents may be to see their adult child marry, however much they gain, they also have to accept a shift in the primary bond of kinship, and they have to share loyalties.

There are few parents who do not wonder: "How much will I lose?" In addition, there are few parents who do not worry: "Will someone else care for my child as he (or she) deserves to be cared for?" There are few parents who do not combine these questions—one "selfish" and the other protective—to justify their strategies as they seek reassurance and stave off loss.

Love: It's Demanding

Love can be approached as a series of expectations as to how someone who loves us will behave. Love can be framed as a series of questions:

"Will you stand by me?"

"Am I special to you?"

"Will I have what I need from you?"

"What will I lose if I have to share you?"

Normally, in a loving relationship, reassurances are given daily, easily, unthinkingly in the course of mundane interactions. These reassurances help us contain our regret at the necessary losses involved in change. For example, young adult children check in with their parents, drop by, ask for help, share their news; the message is, "I'm grown up and independent, but I still love you and need to feel close to you." But sometimes these reassurances are not enough. Sometimes one necessary loss coincides with another necessary loss, and each magnifies the other.

A parent becomes a parent-in-law alongside other midlife changes, and these may also feel like losses. A generalized anxiety about losing power, control, and value will affect the skill and grace with which any single change is accepted.

The fear of loss and the longing to be loved are the most common sources of in-law conflict. The mother-in-law and daughter-in-law may each feel that the other is asking too much of her, or taking too much from her; each feels the other is edging her out of some precious interpersonal center. Neither is content with the son's or husband's allocation of love and attention and company; each feels betrayed, and neither can name that betrayal because it is shaped by an unconscious story of what a relationship should be like. Neither person uses a measure of fairness that makes sense to the other. So, each resents what the other gets and is bemused by what the other wants. What, indeed, does she want from me?

Useless Competition

Ashley acts out her anxiety about loss by testing Jon's responsiveness to her demands. Melissa is disappointed that Ashley is not thrilled to welcome her as a daughter, and that she fails to appreciate what she is bringing to Jon's life. Melissa retaliates by trying to limit Ashley's role in their lives. Jon tries to hop from one relationship track to another, rather than finesse a close but new relationship with his mother. Instead of juggling his different roles as son and husband successfully, he leaves each woman feeling betrayed by the other. From Melissa's perspective, Ashley's need for reassurance takes time and attention away from her. The relationship then becomes framed as a competition.

In this context, Melissa feels she is expected to share more than she wants to share. She even begrudges Ashley her special memories of Jon as a child: Melissa wants to establish her love as the primary love in her husband's life. "I try to show Ashley that we are a couple. I go into overdrive to do this, partly because I sometimes feel Jon's trying to play that down. I like showing Ashley how well I know Jon. Sometimes I feel jealous of how much she knows about his past. Jon's told me about all his other girlfriends—I think!—so they are a part of the Jon I know. But I'll never know him as a little boy. I bet he was adorable! But that's not part of the Jon I have."

Jon tries to keep each woman happy, but ends up making each miserable vis-à-vis the other. To his mother he says, "Nothing between us will change." To his wife he says, "We are not really affected by my mother." Each woman is confused by Jon's (implicit) message, and confusion makes each woman insecure.

The insecurities of each woman are enacted in a competition neither can win.

Abbey, Donna, and Ric:
Anxiety Expressed by Intrusiveness

Intrusiveness is another sign of anxiety over a necessary loss. Abbey, twenty-nine and married two years, launches immediately and forcefully into her complaint about her intrusive mother-in-law:

> Donna drives me nuts. She arrives at our home without ever seeing if it is a good time. She sits down and puts her feet up, like she's stepping into her own home. She goes to the fridge and helps herself to whatever. She'll even cook herself "a little something" and complain about what I have or don't have in the kitchen. Then she'll suddenly notice I'm still around and start criticizing me: if I ate more of this instead of that I wouldn't have such a weight problem; or if I wiped around the sink, there wouldn't be mold on the tiles. It's sort of funny, but it drives me to tears.

In my presence, Abbey is bouncy and forceful. She tells me where to sit when I enter her home. She takes immediate control of the conversation and offers me coffee, all the while entertaining and attending to the thirteen-month-old boy who pulls at her hands, throws toys into her lap, and threatens to push over the floor lamp. At work, she is manager of a team of maintenance workers. She deals with crises in staff turnover and client demands; she oversees staff training and monitors their work. She also has two children—a five year old from a previous marriage and the young son born to her and Ric. Given her obvious skills, the question I blurt out is, "Why do you let her do this?" In other words, why does Abbey present herself as powerless? Abbey ponders this for a moment:

> I sure have tried. But Donna has these *tricks* that pull me in. She says, "Do you mean you're going to keep me from seeing my own son and grandchild?" And I don't want to do that—I don't want to be someone who wants to do that; so I tell her I don't mean that. I tell Ric I don't mean that. So, it's like it's all settled. I can't ask her to respect my home because if I did, I'd be keeping her from seeing her son, or getting to know her grandchild. I keep saying to myself, "Well, I'll let her visit twice this week, and I'll let her stay for much longer than I want her to," and then I think, "Well, now I can ask her to leave because I really have to get her out and just get on with things, and well, just have some time to regroup." So I tell her I really have to ask her to leave, and she says, "Are you really going to kick me out? Are you really going to keep me from spending a little time with my son?"

"I Just Want . . .": Minimizing Strategies

Donna's "tricks," as Abbey calls them, can be labelled *the minimizing technique*. This is the tactic of describing your actions as fulfilling a basic, wholesome, minimal need. In consequence, any objection to your actions is an attempt to deprive you of a basic human need. The person's behavior is contracted to one aim ("I *just* want . . ."). To deny the satisfaction of that wish is surely unfair, unkind, or downright mean, isn't it?

One reason it is so difficult to challenge the minimizing technique is that it is accompanied by a passionate conviction in your own good intentions. Donna in all honesty does not want to intrude; she just wants to see her son and grandson. In fact, she explains to me, "I'm always careful not to intrude. I ask, every time, if she minds me stopping by. Sometimes I visit for just a few minutes, just to check up on everyone, but I never intrude on Ric and Abbey. It's only when I think they won't mind some company that I pop in. It would be nice to feel more comfortable with Abbey. She has this manner . . . Well, she can make me feel very uncomfortable. I know what people say about mothers-in-law. So, I'm very careful. I entertain myself, go shopping, visit a friend, you know, when I have that urge to visit but worry that it's not convenient. I always think, 'Now, how long has it been?' I'm careful not to stop by too often."

Uncomfortable Truths about Love

Love makes us biased, and the self-interest in maintaining connections with those we love can make us blind. Listening to people talk about their in-law problems is sometimes like being spun around and around. Each different perspective looks like an entirely different reality. Emotions roil beneath each conflict; these are felt but not understood. Nothing is simple, no matter how simple it seems.

An uncomfortable truth is that in some of our closest relationships, well-meaning people—even good people like us—tend to be self-interested in assessing what others do. We tend to be greedy in our expectations of others; we tend to be quick to apportion blame to others and slow to see ourselves as blame-worthy. We lose the ability to measure reasonably what we offer and provide versus what others contribute.

This bias emerges clearly in the descriptions that mothers-in-law Ashley and Donna give of their own behavior. They do not get as much love—in the form of time and contact—as they would like; they focus therefore on how much more they would like. They do not see that, from a daughter-in-law's perspective, they are already asking too much, because their experience is that they do not have enough.

Abbey feels she has to make excessive allowances for her mother-in-law, and is driven to tears; Donna thinks her demands are reasonable because she asks for far less than she really wants. Each woman feels edged out by the other. They enact their shadowy, useless negotiations outside the view of the man who is son to one and husband to the other, and who makes light of the conflict. As a result, each woman feels dissatisfied, each feels betrayed.

Spin Bargaining: Searching for Fairness

Donna may play "tricks" on Abbey with the minimizing strategy, but Abbey makes things worse for herself by engaging in a kind of moral bargaining with some phantom, never-to-be-satisfied judge. Abbey's attempts to deal with Donna's minimizing strategy actually make it easier for Donna to manipulate her.

Abbey tries to manage her mother-in-law's intrusions with the loser's game I call *spin bargaining*. This mental gymnastic involves at once resenting a person's accusations and thinking of ways you can absolutely prove that you are free of blame.

You fantasize that, having achieved this impossible position, you will then be able to protect yourself from blame when you refuse their demands.

I call this pattern spin bargaining because it involves making a bargain with your accuser: "Let me prove my innocence and then I'll be cleansed of guilt when I object to your behavior." You try to turn your accuser around by showing how accommodating you are.

Your accuser will never accept your innocence as long as you are objecting to her requests; she will benefit from the bargain you offer, but you will always be spun back around to the starting position. You keep visualizing one scenario after another, and get caught in a cognitive loop that makes you dizzy.

Abbey says to herself, "My mother-in-law is accusing me of depriving her of seeing her son and her grandson. I want to be cleared of this accusation. I'll prove to her I am not doing this by allowing her a great deal of access to them—more access, indeed, than might be considered reasonable. Then I'll be totally cleared of any possible accusation, and I'll be able to say 'no' to her requests."

Abbey disempowers herself with this mental bargaining game. She engages in these mental maneuvers to gain certainty that she is justified in maintaining boundaries of privacy and respect. But she is never going to achieve the certainty she seeks, and Donna has the technique for knocking it flat with, "I *just* want to see my grandson. Are you going to deprive me of that?"

People who are competent in almost every kind of interpersonal forum—as parents, as friends, or in their professional lives—can be at a loss when dealing with in-laws. The failure of our usual interpersonal skills can be so frustrating that we attribute the entire problem to our in-law: "It's not *my* fault that things are going wrong; it's entirely *her* fault. *She's* just impossible." But if we can identify our own roles in in-law problems, we can gain greater control over our domestic lives, and cease to disempower ourselves by demonizing our mother-in-law.

Amina, Partha, and Poorti: Anxiety Expressed Through Disapproval

Amina, twenty-seven and married for two years, was born in England, and describes a childhood in which she sometimes felt completely English and sometimes felt more at home in Delhi than in London. Poorti should welcome her, Amina thinks, as a wonderful daughter-in-law, but she believes that her mother-in-law disapproves of her:

> My mother-in-law was born in India, and her marriage was arranged. It is a happy one, but on a different basis from mine. Partha and I fell in love just like my English friends did. Since I was fourteen I knew no one would tell me who to marry or what to do. That wasn't easy at home, with my own parents. But they are so pleased about how I am and what I am doing. They love Partha. They tease me about what a hard time I gave them when I was a teenager. "You had it all figured out," my father says, "and you let us stew with worry." But all my successes and charms seem lost on my mother-in-law. She seems to think I am very odd. She has said many times that she doesn't believe in love marriages. So I say, "Mama, do you disapprove of me for loving Partha! How could I not love your lovely boy?" Partha laughs, but

my mother-in-law does not laugh at anything I say. She looks
sad. But I wonder whether the problems I have with her are
really about differences in culture. I think the real problem is
she just doesn't want to let her son go.

Amina then lapses into silence. When she speaks again, her
voice has a different, harsher quality. "I feel so much resentment
towards my husband's family because they are so demanding
and because they ignore my needs."

As I talk to people about their in-laws, these shifts from the
openness of exploration and elucidation to sudden coldness
have become familiar. Amina rounds up her description of her
own humorous resistance to her mother-in-law's disapproval,
and her husband's playful responsiveness, with a global criticism of her in-laws. I encourage her to explain, to unravel the
demands they make, and the ways they ignore her needs. She
describes how her mother-in-law "seems deaf around me. I
say something, and whenever I'm telling her something or just
offering a bit of chatter, she makes a polite smile, and clears her
throat, and goes into this heavy sulk."

Amina's mother-in-law, Poorti, explains that she loves her
daughter-in-law, though Amina sometimes scares her. "I know
she is a good woman, and my Partha loves her dearly. But she is
impatient—uhm—you know impatient with me. I know she is
a good woman, but she does not value the things I value. Some
things, yes, but it is a worry that she does not respect what I
respect, and she sees me as something useless. Partha of course
does not say this, but I see it, and it worries me that she will
take his heart away from his mother, and he will lose respect
for me."

Poorti sees her daughter-in-law as wielding a dangerous influence over her son. She sees the differences between them—the upbringing and the values—as a threat to her own position in the family. Will her son continue to respect her? Or will Amina "take his heart away" from his mother and all she has taught him? Amina experiences Poorti's fear as an insult: In the context of that (often unconscious) hope that a mother-in-law will embrace her as a daughter, be thrilled to welcome her into the family, and appreciate what she offers her son, Amina feels frozen out. Her mother-in-law is nonresponsive. She is fearful where she should be appreciative and welcoming. Partha tries to soothe his mother's fears by dismissing them; like Jon, Partha tries to maintain each relationship without changing either.

As a result, Amina explains, "He does a real copout with his mother, by pretending to be a different person with her. It makes me queasy. It's like I lose him. Something goes dead between us when they visit. There's none of that easy comfort. Even private conversation is stilted, because when she's in the house she seems to fill every room. And you can be sure of something else: There's never ever any sex during her visits."

Each woman feels a loss vis-à-vis the other of power, status, and love, and each blames the other for that loss.

The Context of Bias and Suspicion

The earliest references to in-laws in the English language reveal a cultural suspicion of mothers-in-law that persists to this day. A sixteenth-century saying, "Mothers in lawes beare a stepmothers hate unto their daughters in lawes," is cited in the *Oxford English Dictionary* as an example of common usage. But the three case studies in this chapter show that a woman's "hatred" of her daughter-in-law is a complex interaction: Each woman feels threatened; each woman plays a role in the conflict; and each son and husband is distinguished by his emotional absence, an absence that may spring from intense, undifferentiated empathy with both women, making negotiation seem impossible.

The primary source of in-law conflict is anxiety about what we might lose. The pressing questions that so often set in-laws against one another are:

"Will I still be special to my married child?"

"How much will our relationship change, and what will I lose?"

The mother/son relationship during some phases contains an element of romance that sometimes triggers competition when another woman becomes the new closest kin. But if the element of romance that accompanies mother/son bonds were the only explanation of mother-in-law/daughter-in-law conflict, then one would suppose that the father-in-law/son-in-law relationship would be equally problematic. A daughter is as likely to be her father's little girl as a son is to be his mama's boy. Some fathers believe that no other man will care for a daughter as she deserves. Yet, statistically, the chance of conflict is far greater between mother-in-law and daughter-in-law than between father-in-law and son-in-law.[6] The reason for this difference lies in the very different relationships that develop between sons and their mothers, and daughters and their fathers.

What Daughters Do Well

Over time, a daughter is generally better than a son at reassuring both parents that her relationship with them as a daughter will continue, that her love for them is special, and that one element in her interpersonal repertoire will be as their daughter, forever. This reassurance reduces the risk of in-law tension.

Another reason there is normally less conflict between either a mother-in-law and a son-in-law, or between a father-in-law and his son-in-law (despite the fact that a father-in-law is giving way to another man in his daughter's life), is that a daughter normally has worked hard during her teenage years to remind her parents that she is independent and has her own mind, and that certain aspects of her life are off limits to them.

Teenage daughters argue more forcefully and articulately with their parents than sons do. Parents complain bitterly about irritable and argumentative teens, but this vital conflict actually serves a healthy purpose: Such conflicts remind a teen's parents that their child is no longer the little girl the parents may think they know. By the time she marries, a young woman is likely to have already given her parents a crash course in *borderwork*: that is, she gives her parents rigorous lessons in how different she is from them. A daughter, in the cauldron of her teenage years, is also likely to have offered reassurance that though her parents do not always know precisely what she is like, or what she thinks and feels, they are always emotionally connected, for better and for worse.[7]

There are, of course, exceptions. Some women, upon their daughter's marriage, experience a tremendous loss. In one study, a mother of a newly married daughter felt that her daughter had been absorbed not only into a new family but also into a new persona. "Everything's changed. She's a different person, a stranger. I don't know how to act."[8] On the whole, however, women are better at twin-tracking their different relationships as wife and as daughter. In other words, they are more adept at maintaining two different and intense relationships, side-by-side. They offer commonplace reassurances—to both a mother and a father—that they can change, but remain connected. This goes a long way towards reducing a parent's anxiety about losing a daughter when she becomes a wife.

What Daughters-in-Law Do Not Do Well

Why, then, are daughters-in-law not better at getting on with mothers-in-law?

The first reason is that the structure of this in-law relationship is very different from a primary family relationship. Each may be seeking reassurance that she has a special, exclusive role as woman to the man. Each has to accommodate the other, and adjust her needs accordingly. Their man, as both son and husband, tends to be less good at offering adequate reassurances to each woman that she has a secure and special relationship with him, and that each special relationship can thrive alongside the other. He is both bewildered as to what is needed, and may also be unable to express his precious bond to either woman.

The second reason that women have skills to successfully twin-track the roles of daughter and wife, but are less adept at being a daughter-in-law, is that women are aware of the power they have over the men who love them. By this, I do not mean sexual power (though there is that!), but men often hand over a big chunk of executive, moral function to a woman they love. The phrase "my better half" carries real meaning. It indicates significant areas in his life, and in the lives of his children, that are typically given over by a man to his wife.

The domestic moral compass, the family norms, the tributes of loyalty and acts of obligation are usually regulated and maintained by the woman in the family. A mother knows this power, knows perhaps that her son is unaware of this power, and sees her son as giving over a large part of that emotional and executive function to someone else's care. Therefore, a son's mother may understandably be concerned that she is relinquishing more than a daughter's mother relinquishes when her child marries. And so, the common saying "A son is a son till he takes a wife; a daughter's a daughter all her life" signals a deep psychological truth.

A third intensifier of mother-in-law and daughter-in-law conflict resides in the special position that close relationships still play in women's sense of identity. In both early personality formation and cultural legacy, women are more likely to measure and monitor close relationships. They assess the quality of love, put symbolic meaning on many minute acts and exchanges, and take careful note of changes in relationships. In consequence, the following questions are clear and present in many women's minds during life's transitions:

"Will I still be special to him?"

"How much will our relationship change?"

"Will I ever lose him?"

We have only to hear Ayelet Waldman's brutally honest self-assessment to appreciate the depth of the potential conflict: "I pity the young woman who will attempt to insinuate herself between my mamma's boy and me. I sympathize with the monumental nature of her task . . . I sympathize with how much work she faces, but not with *her*. In fact, the very thought of this person, imaginary though she is, sends me into paroxysms of a kind of envy that is uncomfortable to admit."[9]

OVERVIEW

Sharing love is not easy, and the primitive panic of losing a relationship you treasure can turn ordinarily good people into difficult in-laws. The symptoms of this vulnerability-driven conflict are many and varied, from the almost comic-book case reported by Jenny, twenty-six, whose mother-in-law had emailed her two months before the wedding to say, "What you don't realize is that my son thinks about me every day, every minute of the day, every second of every minute of the day," to the more common or garden-variety symptoms such as

- turning a "short visit" into an extended stay
- constantly dropping by without invitation or warning
- routinely having domestic emergencies that involve practical help from a son or daughter
- using the minimizing accusation technique ("I just want something that's right and normal: Therefore, you cannot fairly deny my requests")
- responding to a decline of any invitation or proposal with dismay or even grief (*every* request or invitation is seen as a test of loyalty, so any failure to comply completely is seen as a betrayal)
- regularly criticizing a daughter-in-law to her son, thereby testing the extent of the son's loyalty to his wife

• regularly criticizing a daughter-in-law directly, but not in the presence of her son, thereby surreptitiously establishing a special critical stance that no one else can object to, because no one else sees it

In response, a daughter-in-law may increase the mother-in-law's anxiety by
• being cold or critical of her mother-in-law
• begrudging any time or attention given to her in-law
• reminding her of the primary bond between the couple and minimizing the son/mother bond

The following syndromes ensue:
• *spin bargaining and minimizing strategies*
     You want to establish your own blamelessness *and* be able to set boundaries (as a daughter-in-law); or you want to establish your own blamelessness and assure yourself of connection (as a mother-in-law). So you bargain with some all-seeing judge: "If I allow her this much, then that will be enough; I can say 'no' to her and still be utterly blameless."
     But this position cannot be assured. You will be outmaneuvered by the minimizing technique: "I'm only asking for this small, reasonable thing; you are unfair to deny me this."

• *loyalty competitions*
     A mother, afraid that she will have to relinquish her status and connection when her son marries, sets up tests to gain reassurance of her son's continued loyalty. A daughter-in-law, profoundly disappointed that her mother-in-law does not appreciate what she brings to the family, edges her mother-in-law out of the couple's life.

EXERCISES
for Managing These Primary Conflicts

• Show appreciation for what she (daughter-in-law or mother-in-law) offers her son or her husband.

The three pairs of women described in this chapter could have their relationships turned around if they reassured one another by expressing appreciation for what each brings to the family. Melissa could be proactive in setting up meetings with her mother-in-law, but on her own terms. She could invite Ashley to their home in Chicago; she could set aside occasional weekends where she and Jon would visit Ashley together. In this way, she would assure Ashley of the family connection, while gaining some control over its expression.

Abbey could find times when it would be helpful to her to have Donna in her home. She could ask Donna to get some groceries on her way to visit and encourage Donna to get what she would prefer to eat. And she could say, "I cannot see you now; it would be better for everyone if you came back another time." But she needs to name the time, thereby showing that Donna is not being cast out.

Amina could show respect for Poorti's knowledge. For example, she could ask her to teach her how to cook a traditional Indian meal. She could also show her willingness to be part of the family by aligning herself with Partha's sister or sister-in-law—just to show Poorti that she is not rejecting the entire family.

All three women would be helped by a partner's willingness to express in his mother's presence his love and loyalty and respect for his wife. When a son shows his mother, explicitly, that he and his wife are a couple, her behavior will change. A wife can help her partner do this:

• Assure your partner that he can set boundaries without being disloyal to his mother.

Melissa could suggest that she and Jon always visit as a couple, that he try praising Melissa to his mother as a way of sharing his feelings with his mother (and thereby diffusing the competition, and signalling that any complaints about his wife are a disloyalty to him).

Ric could tell his mother that he is disappointed she visits when he is not at home. He could ask her to cook for them and shop for them (occasionally). This would assure Donna that he is willing to see her, and would also discourage her from the intrusions on his wife.

Partha could assure his mother that he continues to respect her and her values. He could also praise Amina in his mother's presence to remind Poorti that he appreciates both women.

• Keep in mind that the power of in-laws can be managed if the competition formed by fear of loss and disappointment can be turned into collaboration.

When the boundaries of each person are respected, the family is not separated but more comfortably incorporated. The best way to encourage an in-law to accept boundaries is to show that there are perks in accepting the integrity of the couple.

A couple can celebrate a parent—not by always complying with the parent's demands, but by taking the initiative to assure her she remains included in the new family. You can invite her out to dinner, call her to deliver family news, offer her a special invitation to some family gatherings.

You and Your Partner

You and your partner may each have a very different idea of what a couple is. One of you may see a couple as self-contained. The other may assume that a couple routinely includes many others. What seems intrusive to one will not seem intrusive to another. If you argue about what counts as intrusion without having some sense of the definition, you won't get anywhere.

You may have to compromise: Be clear about what you'll accept. If going to a mother's house every weekend is not acceptable, then decide what is, and explain why. Of course you'll have to deal with potential resistance, and slip-back.

Change isn't easy, but it is always easier to act early to instigate change. When patterns are set, change is much more difficult, and people see less reason to allow change. If, over a period of time, a person has managed to get the responses she wants by acting in a certain way, then it is far more difficult for her to change. She will continue using familiar methods to get the rewards she is used to. Learning to get along with in-laws involves learning and teaching the benefits of change.

3.

Are You Really Part of My Family?

Insiders and Outsiders

MARRIAGE is a feature of all known societies, and so are the complicated kinship patterns that arise from marriage. In-law conflict occurs when marriage transforms outsiders into "in-laws," who then have an uneasy status as both insider and outsider.

Marriage to outsiders—that is, to people without close genetic links to us—is a way of preserving the family and ensuring its future; but an outsider also poses a threat to the cohesiveness and "purity" of the family. Some societies try to avoid this dilemma by seeking partners within the pool of close relations. For example, in some cultures, the perfect marriage partner for a son is considered to be the mother's brother's daughter.[1] This marriage between first cousins, called "cross-cousin marriage," is thought to be more stable, less likely to break up on "frivolous grounds" than a marriage between two people who are not already bound by family ties.[2] As with many beliefs about blood and bonds, there is no evidence to support this assumption, but the practice, which remains popular in some cultures, does prevent outsiders from joining the family.

Marrying a close relative is largely unacceptable in the Western world today, but until around the year 300 CE, it was the norm throughout Europe. Marriage to a kin ensured that a family, and the family's property, were secured by people who shared a bloodline. An unmarried man whose married brother died might be obliged to marry his brother's widow in order to prevent his brother's children, and his brother's property, from being claimed by an unrelated husband.

During the fourth century, the laws of the Old Testament that ban incest, and set down broad definitions of incest, were endorsed by the Catholic Church. Some scholars argue that the church's laws were backed by financial motives; it feared that the practice of marrying kin would strengthen a family's position and secure and increase long-term wealth; in consequence, some families might come to challenge the strength and wealth of the church.[3] Whatever the motive behind these laws, the taboo on incest, in its broadest sense, has spread far beyond Christianity and Judaism, and has support from genetic research that demonstrates the benefits to a family of a diverse gene pool and the risks of a smaller one. Though some research now challenges the extent of such risk, marriage between relatives is generally considered unacceptable.

The Role That Sexual Attraction Plays in Potential In-Law Conflict

Cultural norms now prohibit marriage to blood relatives, yet parents nevertheless prefer a son's or daughter's spouse to be "one of them," and they balk at a spouse who in their view does not "belong." Families remain concerned about a family "fit." But the younger generation has a different agenda, with a solid evolutionary aim. The reproductive benefits of marrying outside the family seem to be factored in to the forces of sexual attraction. In studies exploring our responses to other people's scent—known to be a factor in sexual attraction—people are more likely to be attracted to the smells of someone from a different gene pool.[4]

On a psychological level, too, attraction is often triggered by difference, by lack of "fit." According to family therapist Robin Skynner,[5] people are likely to marry someone they see as filling a gap in their primary family. We may be on the lookout, when we sift through our interpersonal world for a mate, for someone who does not fit our family type. Instead of looking for someone just like our closest relatives, we look for someone who complements our family by providing the qualities, the outlook, the personality we felt missing in our own. This would make it more likely that we would choose someone who other members of our family might find strange, or an odd fit. The secret forces of sexual attraction increase the likelihood of in-law conflict.

To make matters worse, the evolutionary biases of parenting increase the likelihood that in-law conflict will lead to marital tension. If a couple have interests only in each other as genetic contributors to their own children, and as protectors of their own children, then their evolutionary interests coincide. They will work together, with no competing genetic claims, towards their own well-being; each focuses on the needs of those in the primary family—self, partner, and their children. When the claims of others with whom one has no genetic interest oneself, such as an in-law, come into play, then love and duty divide a couple. "Why should family resources be diverted to someone with whom I have no genetic links?" our evolutionary selfishness demands when we see our partner offering too much time, care, or attention to a parent-in-law or sibling-in-law.

Steven Pinker wryly notes that from an evolutionary point of view, it comes as no surprise that in-laws rate among the three major causes of marital strife. Infidelity, which threatens one's own genetic connections to one's spouse's children, and stepchildren, who lay claim to family resources but with whom one has no genetic connection, are the second and third of the three major causes of marital conflict; and the issues of stepchildren and infidelity are also big issues in in-law conflict.

Genes are selfish. This does not mean that people are selfish, but behavior that favors and protects those who carry our own genes serves an evolutionary purpose.[6] However fair we hope we are, however good-hearted we believe we are, psychology has evolved along with other human functions in ways that foster the successful survival of our genes. In short, evolution plays a role in making us favorably biased and particularly generous towards those who carry our genes. We are less favorably biased and less generous towards those who might have interests at odds with ours.

Someone who is close to you, with influence over your genetic offspring but not themselves genetically linked to you, will be carefully, suspiciously observed. This is the genetic force behind in-law conflict. There is, in effect, a hardwired resistance to accepting in-laws.

So, while a young Romeo Montague is likely to be attracted to an outsider such as young Juliet Capulet, the parents of Romeo and the parents of Juliet want their child's partner to be someone they consider part of their family—if not genetically linked to their family, then at least somehow "like them." Similarities such as race, religion, ethnicity, and economic and educational status take the place of genetic connections in assessments of "belonging to the family." Parents and siblings test out family fit whenever they are confronted with a potential in-law. The need to continue the family, alongside the threat of bringing an outsider into the family, pose an enduring dilemma to family life.

Common Strategies for Managing the Dilemma

Each set of parents will have a primary interest in their own genetic line. This chapter explores two specific ways these interests are expressed. One common strategy is to control the in-law by reinforcing their outsider status. If you are on the receiving end of this strategy, you are likely to feel marginalized, excluded, and disempowered.

A second strategy is to reshape the in-law into a "fit." If you are on the receiving end of this strategy, you are likely to feel that someone is trying to control you or boss you around; you may endure constant criticism and correction until you become "one of us."

Real inclusion, of course, involves acceptance of who you are, and respect for your thoughts and wishes; so the challenge in confronting either of these strategies is to smash the assumption that you do not belong to the family and that you have to change in order to belong. The case studies in this chapter show why this is difficult, but how it can be done.

Jess, Felipe, and Brisha: Branding the Outsider

Jess surprises me with her opening remark: "I'm your typical all-American girl," she says in response to my question about her relationship with her in-laws. She hears the oddity of her own words, and adds quickly, "That's not how I generally describe myself, but that pins down the contrast with Felipe's family.

"Felipe's parents wanted him to marry someone like them, a nice Philippine, maybe a daughter a close friend would bring to their home. For years they must have been looking over every little girl at every neighborly get-together, sussing out whether she'd be the dark-eyed sweetie for their Felipe."

Often when people talk to me about their in-laws, they use a distinct tone of voice, weary with long-term anger or arch with comic disdain. There is frequently something fixed about descriptions of in-laws: for example, an in-law is described as "always doing this" or "never allowing that" or "refusing every suggestion." I have learned to wait for a follow-up as the near-caricature sketch is either modified or filled in.

Felipe, Jess explains, had talked to her at length when they were first dating about the pressure his family put on him to marry someone "like them." In one of the interviews he agrees to join, Felipe describes that pressure. Five years before meeting Jess, when he was age twenty-two, he fell deeply in love with a woman he had met through his work, but the romance had died through the pressure of his parents' disapproval.

"Everything that happened was somehow a reason why it wouldn't turn out, you know, with me and this other woman.

You wouldn't believe—it makes no sense, but there it was, everything was always a sign that she was wrong for me. My sister is showing our mother a necklace her husband gave her, and mom turns to me and says, 'See, you have to be a couple like your sister and Adan to be a real family.' Or we'd get a phone call from my uncle, and my mother would ask me to pick him up from somewhere, and when I was leaving—she'd sort of hug me and coo, and say I was too good a son to marry someone who couldn't be part of this family. And—well—sometimes it was stuff that just had no connection. Something burned in the kitchen, and I'm helping my mom and sister clean up, and my mom says something about how this is why you marry your own kind. That's just how she sees things. She's a good person, don't get me wrong, but that's how she sees things."

Jess and I are both quiet while Felipe brings his confusion and embarrassment under control. "I couldn't keep that one going. You know, I was young, too. That girl was nice—not as nice as Jess of course. But then, at the time, I really liked her. Really liked her. But it just got too much, this constant . . . 'You'll never be happy. It will never work out. We won't be a proper family.' So, when I knew I wanted to marry Jess, I thought, I don't want to let this go. No way am I going to let this one go. But, well, how do I do it?"

When Felipe introduced Jess and her three-year-old son to his family, he told them that she was "just a friend." His parents would get to know her, he assured Jess, and then they would be okay with the idea of their marriage. His sister would like Jess, and she would help him convince his parents to accept Jess. "Just give them time," he told Jess. "They will love you, in time. Too soon, and you'll just scare them."

"I saw a lot of them," Jess continued the story. "My son, Toby, was comfortable there, and I got on with his sister, though I'm not sure she was ever going to be the best friend Felipe hoped she'd be for me. But, anyway, I figured Felipe had told them. I thought they weren't saying anything about us being engaged because they were still getting used to the idea. It was only when we starting planning the wedding that I realized Felipe still hadn't told his family that we were getting married. Can you imagine? Three weeks before we were going to be married, and Felipe still hadn't told them."

"I never said I told them. Never told you that," Felipe insists.

"You sure implied you had. You kept saying everything was fine—"

"I can't believe you're still going on about this!"

"Well—the fact is they didn't know till the last minute, and they still blame me for that."

"You two can do this by yourselves," says Felipe. "I have stuff to do."

Jess is silent as Felipe leaves the room. The vibrations of the raised voices subside, and she says, "It's not easy for him to talk about this. His parents were livid when they found out we were getting married, that the date was set, that that was that. We've been married three years now, and his mother is civil to me, but it is clear that she doesn't want me as her daughter-in-law, and she's uncomfortable with me being part of the family. She blames me for what she calls the cover-up. She blames me for marrying him. She blames me for having a child and foisting him on Felipe. She probably blames me for every disappointment in her life!"

"Those weeks before the wedding . . . Everyone was in a state of shock. I was furious, and I cried a lot. Felipe's mother sulked, and didn't talk to anyone. The guys crept around like mice because I'd shout if they said anything. Felipe's sister was mad at everyone, too. I'm amazed the whole thing wasn't called off. I think everyone was too shell-shocked to think of that—to think of doing anything. I was running on some hyper auto-pilot. That sure wasn't how I thought I'd feel in the run-up to my wedding. But I didn't want to let his family win."

On the day of their marriage, Felipe's mother, Brisha, handed Felipe a carefully wrapped present. Jess, standing beside him, hoped this was a sign of reconciliation. As she and Felipe unwrapped it, Jess's heart sank. Inside was a framed portrait of Felipe with his mother, father, and two sisters and brother-in-law. Jess said, "When I saw what it was, I had to sit down. I felt like she'd punched me right in the stomach. His mother was showing him who his real family was. This photo was like some religious icon. It was huge, with these garish colors. I realized fully what bad feeling I was up against. It's awful, hating the mother of the man you love. But that's what I felt. And—well—you see what it does to Felipe."

Always Consider How Everyone Interacts

It seems easy enough to blame Felipe's mother, Brisha. Why can't she just accept the woman her son has chosen?

Listening to people talk about their in-laws is like watching a group of skaters spin around one another. Jess is not simply describing a problem with her mother-in-law, even though that's how she sees it. She is describing an interaction between three people. Brisha's story matches Jess's in some ways, but offers a very different perspective, with different things emphasized:

My son is a good boy, smart, hardworking, the best boy. I know he will be a good husband and father, as good a husband and father as he is a son and brother. It is such a big thing for him to marry, and he is still very young. I know, when his father was his age he was married, but now things are different, and Felipe is young. He's such an affectionate boy. I always thought he would marry someone we could make part of the family, you know. We are American, and so proud that this is our home, but it's important to feel who you are in other ways too. Felipe is a man, and can make up his own mind about things, so we let him make up his own mind.

But to come into our home and pretend she is not a girlfriend—how can you trust someone like that? Felipe is always open with me. As a boy he never lied the way other boys lie. He is a good son, and he would not play such tricks on us. This woman has changed him. She got into our home and found out how to get what she wanted from him.

Both women—mother and wife—protect Felipe from blame: Brisha blames Jess for Felipe's reticence about the marriage; Jess blames her mother-in-law for blaming her, and for refusing to accept that she can be a good wife to Felipe. But it is Felipe who has been unable to present his wife to his mother as a woman he loves and to whom he is connected. The breach in Felipe's management of the mother/son relationship makes it very difficult for Brisha to view her daughter-in-law with warmth or to accept her as family. The women blame each other rather than the son and the husband, whose behavior generates the conflict.

If a son or daughter is unable to renegotiate their relationship with a parent, if a son or daughter is unable to show a parent that they now have loyalties and responsibilities to someone else, and that these new loyalties affect the configuration of the family, then it is easier for the parent to deny that new rules of intimacy are in order. In these circumstances, everyone within the relational triangle will feel betrayed.

Anxiety and Anger

In every marriage, the parents of each person forming the couple will ask themselves:

"Will I still be special to my son or daughter?"

"Will my child still be part of my family?"

"Can I cope with things being different between us?"

"What will I have to give up as a result of this change?"

If a son does not reassure his mother that when he becomes someone's husband, he will continue a strong relationship with her and that he will, at the same time, set boundaries around his marriage, then mother and wife may try to negotiate the turf between them. A mother who feels humiliated by her son's reticence or is fearful of losing him either emotionally (because he loves someone more) or psychologically (because someone very different from her and all she knows is becoming his primary family) may console herself by typecasting her daughter-in-law as a stranger and intruder. In that way, she can blame the distance on her son's wife, the interloper and outsider, and her anger obscures her fear of loss from everyone, including herself.

Conflict Escalates Through Bias

No one likes being an outsider. Imagine entering a family circle and suddenly realizing you are among strangers. You think you are among your own people, but you keep picking up signals that you are unwelcome, or that you don't know their rules of behavior. The experience is deeply uncomfortable. However strong we may think we are, however determined we are not to care about the opinion of someone who is unfair to us, we are likely to register social exclusion, and feel great discomfort.

When we are in a social situation and we pick up signals of disapproval or exclusion, our body responds physiologically: muscles tense, pulse rate and blood pressure increase. The body is primed, alert to danger. This is not a state in which we give others the benefit of the doubt.

Jess admits, "I'm constantly waiting for my mother-in-law to say something that offends me. I know something's coming. I prepare myself, because I'm afraid of that swoosh of anger that'll come if she says something that takes me by surprise. Instead, I'm ready to pounce on even the littlest slight. Yes, I know, I know . . . I'm being unfair."

Brisha, too, is poised to be unfair. The introduction into the family of someone who, according to our naïve sociological radar, is "not family" triggers an unease that can make us aggressive and simple-minded.

It may seem odd that we can be more tolerant, more appreciative of differences in people we barely know, than we are of family members. But an in-law whom we see as a stranger in the midst of our family sets off a mental alarm that activates stereotypes.

Stereotypes are simplified mental files, or *schemas*, that the mind uses to process experience. Mental schemas allow us to recognize different individual things as the same sort of thing, and help us use past experience efficiently. They allow us to form expectations about what things do and how they are likely to behave. But when we use schemas in personal interactions, we may make a lot of assumptions on the basis of very little evidence. When we feel uncomfortable, insecure, and confused— as we do in the presence of an observant and disapproving in-law—we are more prone to the simplistic responses shaped by stereotypes.

The naïve sociologist inside each of us is particularly alert where kin networks are concerned. Thinking about who is included in our family is an emotional issue. But in most modern cultures, we have no say in who our in-laws are. Whether we are meeting a daughter-in-law or a mother-in-law for the first time, the naïve sociologist in us may register that the person we are meeting is not our "type," and we are then primed to exclude and disapprove of them. When you add into this mix those deep expectations that one's new family will embrace you and appreciate what you bring to them, you have conditions for the perfect in-law storm.

Accepting Distance Within a Family

In daily social life, marking our distance from other people can be as important in getting along as staking out connections and aligning ourselves to others. We have to know how close, and at what distance, to keep ourselves in order to make others feel comfortable. Without always being aware of our finesse, we set different appropriate distances as we engage in conversation. We position ourselves one way when we speak to our boss, and another way when we speak to a subordinate at work, and another way when we talk to a friend. We signal readiness to get closer, or not, even in casual conversations. When the person we speak to leans towards us, steps close, or in any other way encroaches on our sense of personal space, we have a myriad of ways to reestablish boundaries. We regulate social and emotional intimacy with posture, tone of voice, and eye contact. We know how to invite and to cut off shifts in intimacy. Every day, in commerce, at work, among our friends, we skillfully set and release personal boundaries.

In families, such interpersonal markers can be more difficult. When we set firm personal boundaries between ourselves and someone in our family, our customary social finesse deserts us. Wanting to distance ourselves from a member of our family takes a lot of energy. We are in the position of having already lost ground, because relatives are de facto intimate. To distance an insider, we tend to adopt less gracious maneuvers than we use in marking out our personal distances among non-kin. We may become surly, or hypercritical, or irritable. Then, as we justify our behavior to ourselves, the conflict escalates.

Once we behave unfairly towards someone, a self-protective mechanism is likely to be triggered that heightens our perception of the other person's flaws. To justify our own unkindness, we harden our conviction that the person we show unkindness to deserves to be treated badly. This is one of several *self-justifying principles* that people often use to bolster their sense of being "in the right."[7] This mechanism protects our ego but increases the difficulty of resolving in-law conflict.

Here is a diagram showing how this unhappy cycle reinforces itself:

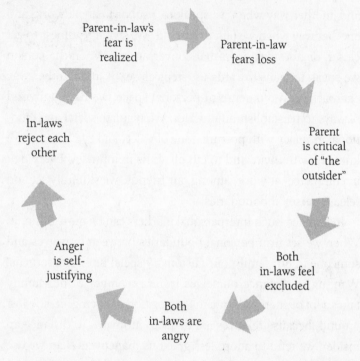

The fear of having to relinquish a valuable relationship makes a parent critical of the person who threatens her. The son-in-law or daughter-in-law then experiences a sense of exclusion, and responds with anger towards the parent-in-law. This anger hardens and self-justifies, so the daughter-in-law distances herself (and thereby threatens to distance her partner, too) from the parent-in-law. The parent-in-law feels justified in being critical of the "unsuitable" spouse who does not belong in her family; after all, she is "cold," which may also mean "uncaring." In consequence, the couple keep their distance from the parent-in-law, and the parent-in-law's fear is confirmed. Yet this vicious cycle can be broken at any point.

Resolving the Dilemma in Three Different Ways

When an in-law does not "fit" into our version of "my family," there are three common responses. The first is to explore and enjoy the differences, and see them as expanding what the family offers. This is Glen's approach to Annie's family: Glen feels

> a real joy in my in-laws' home. Annie's family are like a clan. Their exuberance, when they're all together, scared me at first. Their voices get so loud, and there's always a lot of laughter, and I don't get all the jokes. Sometimes I'm afraid they might be laughing at me. But her folks are so good-natured, and optimistic and enthusiastic about everything. I can't help feeling good in their company. Sometimes I have to pinch myself to realize this is really my family too, and I'm so glad my children will have them as part of their own family.

A second response consists of hurt pride and heightened alarm about strangers in our midst. The overlapping family is offended that a son or daughter has chosen someone so unlike them. They disapprove of their child's partner, or feel uncomfortable in his or her presence. They broadcast messages of social exclusion, which increase the discomfort of everyone and set up a cycle of conflict.

A third strategy is to put an in-law through a crash course in becoming a family member, so that he or she will be "like them." Here the messages of exclusion and inclusion are mixed: "I want to include you in my family, but on my terms." Before we look further at these contemporary case studies, it is worth looking at the solutions practiced in some other cultures.

Rules of Distance in Some Other Societies

Many cultures troubleshoot in-law conflict with rigorous social rules. Some of these rules are likely to strike us as at once bizarre and clever.

The group of practices called "mother-in-law avoidance" prevents conflict by strictly rationing contact. According to these rules of etiquette, a son-in-law is not permitted to sleep in the home of his mother-in-law. In some tribes, there is even a taboo against stepping into the home of a mother-in-law. Contact between son-in-law and mother-in-law is so strongly prohibited that custom demands him to turn his face away from her should he happen to meet her during a sojourn in the village. A wife's parents might visit the couple, but they stay in a special hut for in-laws that sits just beyond the border of the husband's property.[8]

These rituals control contact between in-laws. They also mark the position of the "real," or privileged, family. A wife's original family, and that family's customs, are excluded from the family formed by marriage. Where Brisha gives Felipe a formally constructed family portrait as a means of marking the "real family," from which the wife is excluded, the people living by Bugandan tribal customs have a ready-made ritual for marking boundaries between one family of influence and significance and the other, marginalized family.

In-law avoidance preserves the peace by separating families. The cycles of conflict we see today highlight the difficulties that arise when families overlap and there is no social rule book. In most contemporary societies, different families have to accommodate one another, but there are no rules to facilitate adjustment.

Annie, Glen, and Gaynor: Transforming an Outsider Into an Insider

While Jess feels uncomfortable because her mother-in-law does not acknowledge her as a family member, Annie is uncomfortable because her mother-in-law, Gaynor, is too eager to make her "a real daughter." Annie's mother-in-law embraces her as a daughter on one level, but rejects her as an outsider on another level.

> My mother-in-law says she loves me like a daughter. She wanted a million wedding photos of just me and her. She wanted her daughter as my bridesmaid, and got very upset when I wanted my friend from college, instead. Lately, she is behaving as though she wants to bring me up again, and tries to re-teach me all sorts of things I already know how to do, from cooking to putting on makeup. Here I am, age thirty-seven, and she wants to see my thank-you notes before they go out. She asks me to call her friends "Mrs. So and So" because she wants the "kids in *her* family" to treat elders with respect. It's as if she thinks I'm potentially good, but need to be brought up all over again by her.
>
> Within two weeks of our marriage Glen's mom started "visiting" us and running the house as if it belonged to her. She's made it clear she *has* to visit often to make sure I am properly trained to look after my husband. She rearranges the

furniture. She tells me what Glen should wear. She instructs me how to carry out simple household chores. When I complain to Glen, he tells me that's just how she is, that she doesn't mean anything by it.

Two conflicting messages emerge from Gaynor's exuberant responses to Annie. She embraces her daughter-in-law and celebrates the relationship, in part, by having photos of "just the two of them." But she also indicates that Annie is unacceptable to her as she is. This confuses Annie, who feels that Gaynor is responding to an idea of who her daughter-in-law should be, rather than to the person she is. Annie explains, "I feel unreal when I'm with her. False and dead. I'm a doll."

Like many of us, Annie has a stubborn need to be accepted for who she is. This explains why an adolescent tone so often emerges when a daughter-in-law speaks about a mother-in-law. A daughter-in-law is resisting being judged on someone else's terms; she declares her right to be herself, with her own idiosyncrasies and rough edges, just as she might have done with her mother during the teenage years. At that time, a teen shakes her mother out of old habits of seeing her, forcing her mother to realize that she may not want to be the "good" girl her mother wants her to be.

A mother weathers these adolescent quarrels, and often responds positively, because she does want to get to know her daughter as she really is. For a mother-in-law, however, forging a genuine relationship with a daughter-in-law may not be her priority. Instead, her priority may be to make her daughter-in-law into someone she would like as part of the family. This makeover strategy—trying to reeducate the daughter-in-law to fit the family cloth—is sometimes conducted by constant criticism. Annie says that her mother-in-law makes deeply wounding comments—about her hair, her weight, her glasses, her posture—and "instructs" her on what to eat and how to cook. "She then pats me, hard, on the back or shoulder; it's like a spank disguised as affection."

Seeing Double

In-law conflict will not be quelled until each person involved is able to catch sight of her own biases and distortions. The most difficult lesson is that, when it comes to in-laws, most of us let self-interested passions weight our measure of fairness.

Many people locked in in-law conflict are at some level aware of their own biases. This awareness fills them with self-doubt and misery, so they try to convince others that they are right and the other person is wrong—and these futile attempts again increase the conflict.

When we are angry and feel bad about our anger, we turn to others in our intimate group for help in defending ourselves against criticism. When, for example, we come home from work and describe how someone complained about our management style, or objected to the way we carried out an instruction, we do not expect our partner to say, "Oh, that's just how your colleague is. He didn't mean anything by it. There's no reason to be upset." We want our partner to be angry on our behalf, and reinforce our sense of outrage. We expect our partner to line up, speedily, on our side. A refusal to step into alignment leads to a sense of betrayal, and a bitter argument.

Yet when Glen hears from Annie that his mother criticizes

her, undermines her, disrespects her, he says, "That's just Mom's way. She doesn't mean anything by it." As a son, he does not step up to defend his wife, nor does he offer understanding. Instead he tries to avoid conflict by denying there is any cause for complaint. So, Annie feels betrayed. Her husband is not helping her deal with her anger by confirming it. His response—"That's just Mom's way. She doesn't mean anything by it"—sends the message to Annie that he thinks she is the one at fault: She makes a complaint when there are no grounds, in his view, for complaint.

A partner cannot mediate conflict between a spouse and a parent unless he or she is able to see double—to see both a parent's perspective and a partner's experience. This double vision is difficult because it means stepping back from behavior you take for granted as normal, and looking at it from an outsider's perspective. This double vision is uncomfortable, because it means being critical of someone we love, and that makes us feel disloyal. Yet managing in-law conflict is a job for both members of a couple.

The Closed System of Conflict

"She criticizes me" and "She judges me" are frequent complaints a daughter-in-law makes of her mother-in-law. Criticism has many facets. One of them is care and concern, and Gaynor emphasizes these as she assumes the role of mother as teacher: She will make Annie into her daughter. She instructs her on skills such as rudimentary cooking; she instructs her how to behave in social situations in the way Gaynor would like someone in her own family to behave; and then she offers criticisms that are partly rejection and partly correction, particularly about her weight and clothes.

Her mother-in-law wants to induct Annie into the family rules, but her criticisms mark Annie as an outsider and in the wrong. Gaynor may not intend to send this message, but this is what Annie hears.

Annie responds to her mother-in-law's control partly with reference to her own mother (who loves her just as she is) and partly with her own natural-born pride. As a grown woman, Annie does not want to be taught how to behave by a parent figure who seems to forget that she has already grown up. She becomes angry and irritated in the confines of this relationship. She expresses this irritation to Gaynor, who then finds more to correct in Annie's behavior. Annie's irritation grows, and her behavior towards Gaynor becomes more abrupt.

A COMMON human defense mechanism—a pattern we follow to avoid mental discomfort—is the *self-justifying principle*. When we are aggressive, we justify ourselves by exaggerating the other person's flaws. When Annie expresses irritation, she goes on to convince herself that her mother-in-law richly deserves her abrupt words or her coldness.

Gaynor, however, is likely to emphasize her innocence. She has defense mechanisms, too. Her response is likely to be shaped by the minimizing principle: "I was only trying to help you. I was only trying to teach you. I only want us to be like mother and daughter. My words come from goodwill, kindness, and love." On the basis of what Gaynor believes about her own motives and aims, Annie seems not only unfair, but downright mean to describe her behavior as she does.

"What do you want from me?" is a cry of fear. The consequences of Annie's wounded pride and anger are terrifying, for a
mother-in-law is all too aware, on some level, that her daughter-
in-law has the power to edge her out of her son's life. The diagram below shows another reinforcing cycle of in-law conflict:

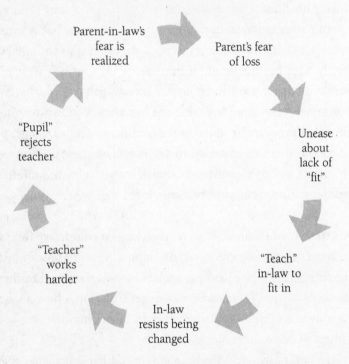

A parent's fear of losing her son makes her sensitive to the differences between her and her daughter-in-law. She tries to teach
her daughter-in-law how to be one of "them." The daughter-
in-law resists these lessons, so her mother-in-law works harder
to "educate" her. These increased efforts escalate a daughter-
in-law's resistance. She may reject her mother-in-law, thereby

confirming her mother-in-law's fear that her son's partner wants to create a distance between her and the couple.

Old Solutions to In-Law Differences

The perfect solution to the enduring problem of how to incorporate someone from a different family into one's own family was practiced by the Arapesh, who believed a man's future wife must live with his family from childhood. The wife's psychological family, then, would be the husband's, and there would therefore be no clash of families. This achieves what is called homogamy, or a full adjustment to the overlapping family.[9]

Other societies have attempted similar solutions. In China, a child-wife, or *tong-yiang-xi*, might be brought into a future husband's home in order to ensure that she respects the status of her husband's family, and accepts their rules of honor. Among many African and Asian societies, a daughter, upon marriage, leaves her own family forever and lives by the rules of her husband's family. Few of us would find these practices acceptable. Therefore we need other strategies for integrating overlapping families, without denying our differences.

OVERVIEW

Marriage involves bringing an outsider into the family. This arrangement

- ensures the future of the family

and paradoxically

- threatens the cohesiveness of the family

A family may try to resolve this paradox by
- preferring an in-law who is "just like them"
- educating an in-law to become "just like them"

These attempts may make the new spouse feel
- rejected
- criticized
- marginalized

The new spouse may respond by
- rejecting their in-laws
- criticizing their in-laws
- marginalizing their in-laws

EXERCISES
for Managing These Conflicts

Study the two cycle diagrams in this chapter. They show how one person's fear of loss may result in exclusion strategies, which lead to aggression and rejection, and then increase the threat of loss.

If these are patterns you experience, then use your awareness of them to break the cycle. This cycle can be broken at any point.

A parent who fears loss can be reassured by the couple, together and individually, that the bond with the parent is secure.

The key fact is that in-law conflict has its source in vulnerability. If you address your in-law's vulnerability directly, you are much more likely to ease the conflict.

- Enlist your partner's help in showing his family that you are valued, and that they should be eager to get to know you and learn who you are.
- Encourage your partner to tell his/her parents about you, and to speak about you with pleasure and pride.
- Encourage him to indicate that behind-the-back criticism of you is unacceptable.
- Encourage him to express pleasure when his parents do show appreciation of you.
- Practice listening to in-laws rather than assuming you know each other or avoiding each other.
- If your parent-in-law offers to teach you how to do things, you can deflect her in the following ways:
  "I'd love for you to cook for us just as you want. Next time, I'll prepare dinner just like I want."
  "I think you'd look lovely in a skirt like this. It's not a style I feel comfortable in."

In a context of proactive appreciation and engagement, your partner's parent is less likely to feel threatened. It is the threat of loss and exclusion that sets the conflict in motion and leads to this cycle of anger and resentment.

EXERCISES
for Managing a Makeover Strategy

When an in-law criticizes you or "coaches" you to change, here are some possible responses:

"It hurts me when you say I'm overweight."

"I'm generally comfortable with what I wear."

Or

"You're so lucky to have such a lovely figure. But I'll deal with my problem my way."

"I admire the way you dress. But I have my own style."

Encourage your partner to complement you and express appreciation of you in the presence of his family. In this way he can show his alliance to you without being disloyal to his parents.

EXERCISES
for New Parents-in-law

When you want to incorporate a son or daughter-in-law into your own family

- Work on the assumption that your in-law knows how to manage their own life.
- Practice listening, not avoiding—perhaps by inviting them to show you their ways of doing things.
- Assume that differences are complementary, that differences expand your family rather than threaten it.
- Test your biases: If we consistently make the effort to take another's perspective, and respond accordingly, we will be able to replace prejudices with more appropriate and effective responses.[10]

4.

Why Is It So Hard on the Women?

Ideals and Competition

DURING twenty years of research on families, I have observed in-laws who love one another, and in-laws who show immense appreciation for what each brings to the family. I have seen in-laws who demonstrate sympathy and stamina for each other's quirks and demands. I have heard about in-laws who are a source of joy and support. In a myriad of ways, in-law relationships can be filled with love, warmth, and tolerance.

I have also found that any in-law relationship can be difficult in the ways that, for many reasons, only in-law relationships can be—jam-packed with tensions over matters that seem tiny, marked by long-term grudges over passing comments, and triggered by one careless comment or sin of omission. Whether it is a parent-in-law, child-in-law, or sibling-in-law, in-law relationships have their special potential for conflict. But I have also observed that the most heated and persistent problems arise between two women—the wife and the husband's mother. While 15 percent of mother-in-law/son-in-law relationships have some tension, 60 percent of mother-in-law/daughter-in-law bonds are described by some strong negative term, such as "strained," "uncomfortable," "infuriating," "depressing," "draining," "simply awful."[1]

THE INTRACTABLE problems between the two women in-laws—the wife and the husband's mother—arise from their similar positions: Each is the primary woman in her primary family. As each tries to establish or protect her status, each feels threatened by the other. "What will I have to relinquish if I respect your position in the family?" and "Will I retain my importance if I acknowledge yours?" signal a vulnerability that can lead to competition over emotive issues about who has more power and more influence in the domestic sphere.

Vulnerability can make apparently minor in-law conflicts feel like storms in the center of our lives. Concern about power and influence, and about the enduring nature of love, is often acted out between mother-in-law and daughter-in-law in the context of female roles, particularly that of "good wife," "good mother," and, more generally, "good woman." These roles generate questions that emerge in the pressure cooker of family life, questions that we answer, only to find that our long-sought answers require further amendments and refinements. Contact and conflict with our in-laws press upon sore points of doubt and regret, and many women find themselves enacting global battles between cultural ideals and personal realities on their own domestic turf.

The Domestic Watch

Most of the time, most of the women who collaborated with me in these studies assured me that they had little patience with the ideals that may have dominated the lives of women during the middle part of the last century. The mystique of the perfect mother and the ideal wife, for both mothers-in-law and daughters-in-law, signals ideals they are likely to relegate to time past. Nevertheless, these so-called defunct ideals became live issues between mother-in-law and daughter-in-law.

Sammi, Tim, and Marge:
The Emotional Issue of Housework

Sammi, at the age of thirty-four, is normally comfortable with her domestic lifestyle, but a visit from her mother-in-law, Marge, injects her with self-doubt:

> I try to play it cool, and say to myself, "She can just take me as I am." But as soon as Marge steps through the door I start seeing things that ordinarily don't bother me one bit. The homey feel in the living room suddenly looks like a train wreck. Marge is never outright critical, but last time she came she took one sorrowful look around the place and said, "You must be awfully busy at work." I damn near choked on that. What was she doing? Offering me some excuse for the messy house?
>
> I know how important it all is to her. Neat as a pin, she keeps her home. She's always rushing around, muttering to herself as she cleans up. "Let me save you a job," she says, and she picks Tim's clothes out of the dryer and starts folding and smoothing them. Day one, I keep my mouth shut. But day four of her visit, I tell her, "Marge, it's Tim's job to iron his own shirts, so you're not saving me a job, you're saving Tim a job, and I hope he thanks you." I never know if she gets it, or if just one more thing has flown out of my mouth to put her in a sulk. Sure, I should follow Tim's advice and not let it get to me; but that's easier said than done. She presses on

all those sore spots. When she's around, I catch myself worrying: Is my home downright unwholesome? Am I ruining
my kid's life with this environment? Shouldn't—you know—
shouldn't the sheets be smooth and straight? Marge doesn't
have to say much to work my mind to that drill.

Like many women I interviewed, Sammi describes a spike
in self-doubt in her mother-in-law's presence. Though Marge
denies that she is in any way critical of Sammi, she also says,
"Everybody wants a clean and orderly home. When I visit I like
to make myself useful, so I help her with that. I know that's
what Tim wants, too, and it's better for the baby."

Marge is not alone in her assumptions. A survey of one thousand women showed that 80 percent believed that the standard
of cleanliness in a home was an important issue in whether or
not they could warm to a daughter-in-law.[2] In some cases this
may register simple generational differences. Younger and older
women may have very different ideas about what a woman is
supposed to do. Someone who believes that you should have a
dust-free house, a spotless kitchen, and children who look nice
and neat because *you've* washed their clothes will not understand
someone who thinks that her career is crucial to who she is, while
housework is, to her, just a chore.

But the value a mother-in-law may place on a clean home, or
her assumption that the responsibility for household cleanliness
is her daughter-in-law's, does not fully explain responses like
those of Sammi—responses that are common, that deeply affect
the daughter-in-law's contentment, not only with her mother-
in-law but also with her husband, and with herself.

Unwelcome Mental Inhabitants: The Over-Eye

Mother-in-law/daughter-in-law conflict often emerges from an expectation that each is criticizing or undermining the other. As a daughter-in-law, you may believe that your mother-in-law's domestic routines set a standard that you think she expects you to follow. As a mother-in-law, you may think that your daughter-in-law's lifestyle implies criticism of your own values and achievements. This mutual unease may have less to do with actual attitudes, and far more to do with persistent female norms that few of us manage to shake off completely.

In her work with women and depression, Dana Crowley Jack identified an internal, nagging observer, and named it the *Over-Eye*.[3] Social norms are internalized, so that even when we resist them, they may get in our way. For example, the norm that housework is the job of a (good) wife, and that a good home must operate as a clean and neat home, can be activated and make you feel deficient, even when the more conscious and determined part of your mind rejects those assumptions. Cultural associations stick, even when you personally do not endorse them. That is why housework can be so emotionally laden: Who does it well may be a sign of who is caring and loving.

Why Can't You Just Ignore This?

"Why do you let this bother you?" Tim demands. "You have so much going for you. There's no reason to feel she's putting you down. That's just how she is. Just let it go."

Tim reminds Sammi that there are things about *her* parents that bother him, and he just ignores them: Why can't Sammi do the same with his mother?

Ignoring comments is not an option for women dealing with their in-laws. Women rarely have the knack of switching off their antennae. In-law visits take place within the home, and the home is a testing ground for still-powerful questions about women's roles and the symbolic value of domestic acts. Whether it's remembering a nephew's birthday or pouring the milk into a jug before setting it on the table, small, apparently insignificant gestures can take on meaning, or become points over which meaning is teased out. When women of different families become, in law, one family, each can trigger the other's dormant anxieties about norms within the home.

Carol, Gillian, and Paul: Praise as Control

Reminders of female domestic norms can ignite anger that may seem inexplicable and irrational to others. Carol, forty-three, feels threatened by her mother-in-law's praise. "You've done a lovely job on this kitchen. My, those curtains are adorable" and "That pot roast was something else. You just have to tell me how you do it," Carol mimics her mother-in-law, Gillian, and sighs. "And the next thing I know Gillian's talking about her other daughter-in-law, how wonderful she is, how she's done these marvellous things with her children or her house, or how she gave her a super-duper present or said something really nice to her. My husband says that she's just talking, just giving us the family news, just trying to be nice. But you can't convince me it's 'just' that."

Gillian cannot fathom the source of her daughter-in-law's unease. "That woman is ornery," she tells me. "You never know how she's going to jump. No way of knowing what's going to calm her down and what's going to wind her up."

Carol feels criticized when her mother-in-law praises her, because she thinks Gillian's "praise" marks out a hierarchy of values and her own low score on that value system. Gillian is unaware of this possible interpretation, and is unable to crack the code of her daughter-in-law's responses.

"You Raised Him Like This": It's Easier to Blame His Mother

Husbands are under pressure to change—to put more time into running the home and caring for their children, to revise their expectations of a wife's role both within the home and at work, to learn new ways of sharing and connecting. Some men have to unlearn patterns they learned from their parents' allocation of domestic work. Some women, as daughters-in-law, blame their husband's mother for their partner's resistance to change; and some women, as mothers-in-law, feel that a daughter-in-law's complaints about a son's behavior denigrate the domestic habits they themselves value.

At the same time, many mothers-in-law insist that they have done their best to raise sons to be new men, that they have encouraged their son to respect women's careers and to take on a fair share of domestic tasks. They are confounded by a daughter-in-law's view that they have failed.

Lisa, Andrew, and Pam:
Battling Expectations

Lisa, age forty-one, has been married to Andrew for six years.
She complains that even though her career achievements equal
those of her partner on every objective measure, her mother-
in-law sees Andrew's merits in bolder colors, and her role as
supportive and subordinate:

> I'm at the same corporate level as my husband. We get the
> same salary. Yet she's always going on about his work, his
> career. It drives me crazy. And there's always this meta-
> message: "His career is more important than yours, and you
> should put him first."

One consequence of Pam's bias is, Lisa believes, "every visit
from his mother sets Andrew back at least a year in my battle
to make him carry his weight at home. He asks, 'Where's the
butter?' and his mother jumps up and puts it down in front of
him. She doesn't see I'm trying to downsize his expectations of
domestic service."

Pam is hurt that Lisa devalues the roles she takes pride in. "It
took me a long time to figure out what her beef was. She'd hit
the ceiling for the smallest little thing. I couldn't figure it out.
But now I see. Now I get it. She doesn't think I should do what
I've been doing for forty years. She wants to tell me how to treat
my own family. She can't stand it that I put myself out for the
people in my family. Well, what can I do about that? Where can
we go from here? I was a good enough mother to raise a son she
wants to marry. I'm not going to change for her say-so."

In the center of this storm is Andrew, who is guilty if he

accepts his mother's service, and guilty if he resists it. Using a common psychological trick called scapegoating, Lisa bypasses her husband, and blames her mother-in-law for her husband's behavior.

In some cases, it is easier to resent a mother-in-law for "spoiling" her son than it is to resent a husband for failing to do his share of domestic chores. Battles about who does what can have a devastating, cumulative effect on a marriage. When Arlie Russell Hochschild studied couples who began married life determined to share household tasks and child care equally,[4] she discovered that many wives gave up the struggle for the sake of marital harmony. When a wife does not feel that her husband is doing a fair share, she may seek to preserve marital harmony, and moderate her own anger with her spouse, by blaming her mother-in-law.

Maternal Conservatism

When I began my second study of in-laws in 1999, and my third study in 2004, I expected that the generational divide I had first noticed twenty years before would have been bridged.[5] Certainly, women I interviewed as mothers-in-law saw themselves as sharing a cultural shift with their daughters-in-law. They experienced the same pressure to juggle work and family. They shared high expectations of their own achievements across many aspects of their lives. These mothers-in-law were women born in the 1940s and 1950s and 1960s; they themselves worked hard to create an equal partnership with their husbands. So, it was a surprise to hear Angie, age fifty-two, say that she hoped her daughter-in-law would lose her bid for a seat in Congress because her

children saw little enough of her anyway. Angie explains her
position:

> I know from my own experience how important it is to have
> your own career, and develop your skills. I worked pretty
> much all through the time I had my children, and I'm still
> working now. But looking at Steph's drive—well, there's a
> limit. My son Ian has to be home by 5:30 every evening to
> take over from the babysitter. He's the sole parent on week-
> ends. He's not always in good health, with the burdens he
> has already. The youngest child is a real handful. I'm sure this
> acting out is because he doesn't see enough of his mother.
> Can you imagine how things would be for him if Steph's
> elected to Congress? I admire her. I really do. But there's a
> limit to what she should ask of Ian and the children.

While general views on women's roles have changed, in the
role of mother and mother-in-law, a woman's perspective may
be in a time warp.

A mother wants what's best for her son. Doing his fair share
of family work is not necessarily best for *him*. A mother remains
focused primarily on the son's interests, and those interests, in
our society, involve a good career, a well-run home, and leisure
time. A good career depends on long hours at work; contented
children and a well-run home involve constant time and attention. A woman also wants what's best for her grandchildren,
and a mother at home is the most simple way—if not necessarily the best and only way—of meeting children's needs. So
wherever she is intellectually, a mother-in-law's heart may well
lie with a 1950s model of a daughter-in-law.

Most mothers-in-law protest that they do not set domestic

ideals for a daughter-in-law, and do not expect her to fulfil the traditional model of "wife." Many say in all sincerity that they are keen to raise sons to be new men who are as responsive to children and as domestically responsible as their partners. Yet, on a deeper level, they may want a daughter-in-law who puts her husband first.

Mothers of both sons and daughters see their own child as of supreme importance. Each mother wants her own child to thrive, and each mother-in-law has a bias towards the well-being of her own son or daughter, who will always "come first" with her. But when that child is someone's husband, a mother's perspective may also be shaped by the privileged status he's likely to borrow from the remnants of the wider culture (such as the assumption that the man's career comes first). A daughter-in-law has to fight to ensure that her career goals receive equal respect. When these goals are undermined by someone within her own family, she redoubles her efforts to defend them.

Many of the familiar complaints about mothers-in-law are powered by the fragility of women's gains in the public world. They erupt from hypersensitivity to conservative messages about roles in the family. In this context, even a throwaway message that a husband's career and comforts have priority may set off fireworks.

Women dread taking on the mantle of the mother-in-law, with all the accompanying clichés, and they work hard to establish new images and roles. Yet nothing teaches us more about the precarious truce in the war between the sexes than this uneasy relationship between two women. And this clash continues to present a conservative force in family life. When a daughter-in-law expects female support and friendship from a mother-in-law, she feels betrayed by the mother whose son comes first.

Any treaty between mother-in-law and daughter-in-law will depend upon a woman, when she becomes a mother-in-law, taking a broader view of her son's best interests. It will depend upon a woman's skill, as she becomes a wife, to teach both her husband and his mother how to read new scripts of equality.

Role Ambivalence Does Not Prevent Role Competition

There is a further twist to those in-law tensions that spring from domestic roles. Even though many daughters-in-law want to revise male and female roles within the home, they compete with their mothers-in-law to fulfil these roles—as wife and mother, as housewife and kin keeper. They want to prove that they fill these roles as well as, perhaps even better than, their mother-in-law.

Role competition arises on many fronts. The most obvious involves status. A daughter-in-law is an adult in her own household and, as such, is equal to any woman in the family. But a mother-in-law's maternal expertise is well established, and she may expect deference from a daughter-in-law. There then arises that tricky question about who is "mother" in the family, with final say over all those things that women—for all the change there has been—still assume charge over: housework and child care, mealtimes and children's manners.[6]

Sammi complains that her mother-in-law takes over these roles as soon as she enters the home: "She takes charge of the kids. She bustles around, telling them what to do, telling them how to do the things I help them with every day. 'This is how you brush your teeth' and 'This the best way to wash your face' and 'This is how you should look every day before you leave the house.' I have to get myself out of the room quick, otherwise I'll scream."

Carol feels that the running commentary of praise she gets from her mother-in-law sets Gillian up as her judge. "She praises me because she knows better—as though I want her approval. It's a way of lording her status over me." So Gillian's attempt to be a "good mother-in-law" and express her approval of Carol is seen by Carol as a bid for status. Competition between two mothers of different generations makes each uneasy, but for different reasons. Carol and Sammi press up against their own lingering ambivalence surrounding their choices, and their own hovering concern that, in breaking with traditional female roles, they may be harming their husband or children. Marge and Gillian feel their daughter-in-laws' resistance as disrespect to them, as undermining their value as the mother in *their* family.

Women Notice the Tension More

For centuries, women have had special incentives for "reading minds" and monitoring the flow of human interaction around them. Some psychologists argue that this skill arises from women's traditionally subservient position: dependence on others' goodwill and approval has heightened their sensitivity to others' responses. Some psychologists argue that this skill is demonstrated from birth,[7] and that women's natural-born empathy facilitates the roles they have played throughout human history.

Day to day, girls and women spend more time reflecting on what has been said by whom, and on considering the implications of verbal acts, than do boys or men, in general. The kitchen-size exchanges that so often form the fabric of in-law complaints have an exquisite clarity to women, but many men simply do not notice them.

Women tend to be more observant of the myriad of minute expressions of feeling that constitute every interpersonal exchange. When someone is uncomfortable in their presence, or when someone dislikes them, or dislikes someone they care for, women are more likely than men to pick up on this. They set high standards for interpersonal relationships, particularly within the family. They are quicker to step in to soothe a distressed child, to intervene in a sibling quarrel, or to pick up on the indicators of stress or sadness that a teenager might try to hide. Women are also more likely than men to instigate divorce, even though they are also likely to suffer greater financial disadvantage in consequence; the higher standards they set for a good marriage make them willing to risk more by ending an unsatisfying marriage. With their friends, girls and women worry over the quality of their relationships, and brood far longer on the causes of the quarrels, replaying and revising accounts of how a quarrel arose, who said what, who was at fault, and how the quarrel can be remedied.[8]

The special attention women give to interpersonal domestic politics—a skill sometimes referred to as "women's intuition"—is often focused on maintaining harmony and meeting others' needs; but, in the realm of in-laws, this sensitivity promotes hostility as often as it promotes harmony. As women describe uncomfortable interchanges with a mother-in-law, they often describe public acts of rudeness and criticism to which the men in the family are oblivious.

Women Have Special Skills for This Kind of Battle

In describing the overall context of in-law unease, we can see why the power of in-laws affects women more than men. The heated issues that arise within the domestic setting, their high expectations for domestic harmony, their ambivalence about work and family balance, their sensitivity to status in the home are sufficient to explain the special impact these tensions have on women; but the *tactics* so often used in these battles also heighten the discomfort.

The tactics used in many in-law battles have much in common with squabbles on the school ground. Though enacted in a different setting, the tactics are reminiscent of those used in girls' cliques. These schoolgirl cliques are in many ways like kinship networks. The distinctive dynamics of girlhood friendships allow strong alliances to be formed. Girls, in their friendship groups, have high expectations of mutual affection and admiration. These alliances offer support and comfort and protection, but girls constantly negotiate and renegotiate boundaries between insiders and outsiders in the group, just as in-laws do.

Girls engage in *borderwork*, or an exploration of who is "in" and who is "out," who is similar and who is different, with a mix of apparent friendliness and relentless criticism. Much of this criticism consists of gossip, or behind-the-back reports that impugn another girl's motives, character, and behavior in a setting she cannot challenge. Girls also use indirect criticism and innuendo as opportunistic weapons, and they battle over who is "nicer" and who is most popular, or admired, or liked.[9]

The tactics used to exclude and criticize are rarely mentioned by boys in their friendship groups, but they cause girls enormous pain during those friendship wars of junior high school. When the tactics are replayed during in-law battles, they awaken awful memories. Past experience makes women both more skilled in these battles and more uncomfortable with them. While the long-term, low-key, indirect attacks go unnoticed by others, the weapon of disguised, indirect criticism puts daughter-in-law and mother-in-law in the arena of the mean girls they hoped they had long ago left behind.

OVERVIEW

This chapter looks at in-law conflict in a very contemporary social context. But here, too, the familiar guidelines for making sense of in-law problems hold.

First, follow the vulnerability: Who is worried about losing a valued relationship, or status, or influence?

Second, identify the unconscious hope that may be at work: Who is disappointed at not being appreciated for what she brings to the family?

Keep in mind:

- Each of you may be vulnerable to criticism or other devaluing strategies.
- Whether you are concerned with putting in excessive domestic work, or whether you are concerned with being seen as negli-

gent in your domestic work, any criticism is a symbolic attack on your value as a wife, a woman, and a mother.

- Each of you may have (largely unconscious) expectations that you will be embraced by the other as an ideal daughter/ mother.
- At the very least, each expects, on some level, female support and alliance.
- Criticism crushes any expectation of female solidarity; and disappointment can lead to anger.
- Each may be hypersensitive to the other's attitudes because each is uncertain about her own status, or her own values.

EXERCISES
for Managing These Conflicts

- Address your own self-doubt.

    If you feel your mother-in-law is judging you, try to identify the criticism. Then ask yourself, "Is this something I really care about?" If not, put that useless ideal in a box and put it away. If you do care about the criticism, then think in positive ways about how to improve your lifestyle. But don't blame your mother-in-law.

- Identify your own biases.

    If you are a mother-in-law, watch out for the bias towards your own son. There is nothing wrong with caring more about your own son than about your daughter-in-law. There is nothing wrong with a parent seeing her own son's career or comforts at twice their normal size. But if this parental bias minimizes the achievements of your daughter-in-law, it will generate conflict. If this parental bias is openly acknowledged in the context of your love for your own child, it will be accepted.

5. *Whose Side Are You On?*

Why It's So Tough to Get Support from Your Spouse

CONFLICTS within a family carry special complications. When we are at odds with a colleague, we can assess the damage, reset our antennae, and look out for our own interests. When we argue with a friend, we can take time out, and stand apart until wounds mend. We can switch off a friendship temporarily, taking care to negotiate new distance or gradual reconnection. In either case, we seek comfort from our most reliable supporter, our partner, to whom we relate our daily experiences of social bruising and who can always be depended upon to see that we are in the right.

In the thick of family conflicts, such defensive maneuvers are much more difficult. We have to consider constantly other people's feelings, other people's loyalties, as well as our own. In family conflicts, we lose the control we may have elsewhere over the timing of our encounters. Within a family, we cannot avoid meeting as we nurse an insult. To withdraw until we personally are ready for renewed contact would interfere with our partner's and children's expectations.

Worst of all, while these problems arise within the network of people we are closest to, we often feel alone as we deal with them. The people we normally depend on to take our side have other loyalties. They also have other measures of what's normal and acceptable. Nothing increases the frustration of in-law conflict more than a partner's failure to support your bids for what you need in your family.

Marriage creates overlapping families. Each person who forms a couple must be ready to accommodate and include members of that overlapping family. But one basic expectation in marriage is that our partner will be on our side when we are criticized, hurt, excluded, or imposed upon.

We might fight with a partner over big things and small. Arguments, broadly speaking, are part of marriage. In the loose sense of "arguing," we use arguments to negotiate life with another person. Even so, we expect a partner to stick up for us when someone outside the marriage threatens us, criticizes us, makes us feel bad. The last thing we expect, as we tell our partner about the events of our day, is to have him side with someone we're complaining about—a colleague, a friend, a plumber—and say, "The other guy was right." If that happened regularly, we'd give up talking about our day-to-day conflicts and conclude there was something rotten in the state of our marriage. But this, I have found, is precisely what happens, over and over again, when conflict arises between in-laws.

Shelly, Cal, Nora—and Vera: Unexpected Triangles

Throughout the first three years of her marriage to Cal, Shelly found her mother-in-law, Nora, "welcoming and caring." Shelly was confident that she would avoid that old "mother-in-law thing."

I started out thinking: That's just an ugly stereotype. Only women with closed minds and bad mouths would buy into it. Sure, there were things that kind of niggled away. There was the odd cold comment that kind of slid into the conversation, real quick and quiet, and you think "What? What was that snipe all about?" But, you know, a mother-in-law is just a woman whose son happens to get married. She's not some special breed. You'll get your ordinary mix of the good and the bad. I was fixed on that thought. I wasn't going to let it go for just a few slippery comments.

But Shelly eventually reversed "this self-deluded fair and balanced expectation." The turning point was the first Thanksgiving dinner she attended in her mother-in-law's home. When she learned that Cal's first wife, Vera, would be coming, she thought, "This is odd." Cal had told her that Vera was "out of the picture." But, Shelly reasoned to herself, Vera would be coming as the mother of Cal's son, Sean. Perhaps Nora thought it wouldn't be right to exclude Vera, especially if Vera might otherwise be spending Thanksgiving alone. Nora was being polite and kind. "I tried to hold onto that thought," Shelly explains.

Holidays, with their ritual meals and gatherings, are excellent opportunities for family bonding; they also put stress on families, and increase the risk of conflict. Expectations tend to be high: Will this year's be as good as last year? Will everyone have a good time? Family gatherings require a lot of preparation, and some members of the family do more than others. Those who work at it hope to be rewarded, not only with appreciation and gratitude but by seeing other's pleasure and enjoyment.

Some family gatherings foster alliances within the family. This is one of the many ways that holidays and their rituals confirm and maintain a family's togetherness. But, with the excitement of coming together and the anxiety as to how it will all turn out, tensions and divisions also arise. During the course of the day, Shelly felt excluded:

Nora and Vera hung out in the kitchen for hours. They were chatting away like sisters hungry for each other's every word. And these words were private. I went in a few times, thinking they were cooking, just cooking, and that I could help. No room for me, I can tell you. A cold pause gave me the shivers when I swung that door open. Cal said I was just imagining it, but I swear Nora seemed to watch me to see whether I was noticing just how thick she was with Vera. She laughed extra loud at Vera's jokes, and kept hugging and patting her.

That day was a turning point. I notice more and more just how Nora keeps praising Vera every chance she gets. I keep hearing about how she's so successful, and what a great mother she is. Nora's first bits of news are always about Vera and Sean. She visits them a lot. We all live in the same town, which is good, because I really want Cal to see Sean, but this makes things so hard with Nora.

I get a real bad headache the minute Nora launches into one of her eulogies of Cal's ex. What can you do? I just smile like I'm real happy there's this wonderful woman in the world, and try to change the subject. One day I thought I might just try to tell Nora how this made me feel. My thought is: She gets her head round to my perspective, and we're sorted. So, I start telling Nora that maybe there's too much of wonderful Vera in the conversation, and that maybe Vera didn't have to be included in every family get-together.

I knew as soon as I launched into my well-prepared speech that something was going real wrong. Nora went all stiff, and stared at me. I tell you, it was some stare! And then there was some torrent of words I don't want to recall let alone speak out loud. I'm not a timid person, but that switchover to out-and-out rage made me feel sick enough to be scared. The gist was that I was trying to split up the family, that I was a soul-destroying bitch, and such. I was tongue-tied and got out of her home, quick.

I told Cal what happened and he was real sweet. He saw the funny side of it, and the awful side. I was so relieved because at least he was on my side. Then Cal's brother came storming into our house, demanding to know why I had been attacking his mother, how it wasn't my place to speak out like that. Cal calmed his brother down, but then turned to me and said the same thing: "You don't show her disrespect. You don't upset her like this."

Whose side is he on? It was a shock to see him glaring at me like that. I felt sick, a sickness I now call "in-law sickness." Watching someone you think is rooting for you suddenly change sides, without warning, and freeze you out—it leaves you sick and shaken.

Lining Up Loyalties

Loyalty is a touchstone of attachment. Circumstances change, we change, but loyalty remains a fixed bare minimum of belonging. In overlapping families, however, loyalty sometimes fragments into competing loyalties.

Alliances between individuals within a family have many motives and serve many different purposes. Some special alliances are essential to good family functioning. Parents work together to protect and control their children. These alliances are functional; they allow the special parental cooperation that facilitates child care; they also enforce parental rules and policies.

Siblings, on the other hand, are likely to compete over every last thing within the home, but the bonds of identity and love are usually strong enough to activate loyalty on the street outside. Both competition and alliance help the siblings integrate the complex nature of their attachment, which involves both love and rivalry. They compare themselves to one another in order to gain a sharper sense of who each is. As they fight and play and cooperate, they gain skills in living in a world with other people. Both alliances and the conflicts between siblings are, generally, functional.

But daily life in some families is pervaded by bizarre power struggles and power coalitions. One parent, for example, forms an alliance with a son or daughter against another parent. A mother who feels angry and betrayed by her husband might encourage a son to be rude or unruly with his father. Such alliances undermine all family members and replace support with anxiety.

Alliances in overlapping families can be similarly disruptive. An alliance between a son and a mother that undermines the son's wife badly interferes with a couple's equilibrium. Instead of sharing views and offering mutual support, an alliance with a parent against a spouse splits the couple in two. A daughter-in-law feels humiliated, excluded, and undermined, and tries to defend herself by attacking both her husband and his family. If a parent's aim is to avoid losing her close relationship with her son, then she may succeed; but she may also incur the loss of her son's marital happiness.

Alliances and Dilemmas

Nothing is simple in the realm of in-laws. The clear rule to "stand by your spouse" may be obscured by conflicting loyalty to a parent.

Nora, Shelly's mother-in-law, is bound to Vera, Cal's ex-wife, as the mother of her grandchild, Sean. Nora is also fond of Vera. When Vera and Cal were wife and husband, Nora established an independent, vibrant friendship with her daughter-in-law. Vera's and Cal's divorce has not changed this friendship: "I've known Vera for thirteen years," Nora explains. "She's spent every Thanksgiving, Memorial Day, and Fourth of July in this house. I'm not going to bar my door to her just because Cal's decided to leave her."

This sounds reasonable, until the whole picture is considered. In overlapping families, there may be overlapping motives for conflict and loyalty.

Shelly's primary conflict is with her mother-in-law, but it arises from her mother-in-law's loyalty to Cal's ex-wife. Even this does not become "in-law sickness" until she discovers that Cal (in alliance with his brother) sides with his mother against Shelly.

Cal believes he owes his mother his first loyalty: "My mom raised me all alone. She gave up a lot for me, and it's important for me to be a loyal son." Shelly's retort is: "Then why did you bother marrying anyone, if your first priority is your mother?"

Many issues are played out in the midst of these loyalty pulls. They create a white noise that detracts from the central issues. One conundrum is, "Who is being fair to whom?"

Nora thinks that Shelly is being selfish by expecting her to draw a boundary between Vera and the family. Cal remains bound to Vera as mother of his son. He is also bound to Nora, as her son. He also has a bond to his brother, who stands by his mother.

Shelly's resistance is seen by her in-laws, and subsequently by her husband, as a failure to respect these bonds. Shelly can no longer remember what she said, but she is convinced that the version Nora gave to Cal's brother contained "some exaggeration and a whole lot of distortion." In any case, Shelly's concern is not "Who said what?" but "Who stands by me?" Her challenge to Cal is, "I am hurt and you are my husband, so you should stand staunchly and publicly by me." In this context, there is the further challenge, "You have to decide who's more important to you: me or your mother." In the mind-set of competition and conflict, she loses sight of the only viable framework for resolving this loyalty dilemma, which is collaboration.

Framing Dilemmas

Dilemmas about loyalties are at the foundation of Western culture. Should Abraham obey the voice of God ordering him to sacrifice his son Isaac, or should he fulfil his protective duty as father? Should Agamemnon preserve his country's code of honor by sacrificing his daughter in return for a fair wind for his army, or should he protect his daughter Iphigenia? Should Antigone show respect to her brother by giving him the rites of burial, or should she respect her uncle's (and the king's) law? Dilemmas over loyalties create opportunities for the hard thinking and tough action of drama. But they also shape the minute-to-minute acts of loyalty we have to finesse in family life.

Normally we try to avoid dilemmas. When they hit us in the face, we may ignore them and hope they'll just go away. We may try to control the dilemma by trying to control the person we think we can most easily influence. The working principle then is: "If you don't make this demand of me, then I won't have to deal with competing demands." But this control does not resolve anything. Dilemmas can make people clumsy; we act out, counterproductively. Or dilemmas make people lazy; we turn away and withdraw from them.

Resolving loyalty dilemmas is nonetheless key to harnessing the power of in-laws for the good of the family, for strengthening family networks, and for satisfying the abiding need each person has for a close connection to those he has loved from infancy. Cal should stand by his wife, but he also needs to honor that emotionally central alliance with his mother. Cal should stand up for his mother, but also honor that emotionally central alliance with his wife.

To resolve this dilemma, something has to change drastically. The conflict between the couple and the mother-in-law has to be transformed into a collaborative relationship. The son has to realize that he can be loyal to his wife and also be a good son. The wife and daughter-in-law must negotiate a compromise perspective whereby she can join her husband in showing respect to his mother.

Resolving Dilemmas

There are many variations of the "in-law sickness" that Shelly identifies. This in-law sickness marks the brutal switch of alliance from partner to parents. There are four common responses to loyalty pulls, four different stratagems to deal with the demand "Whose side are you on?" Each variation requires a different resolution.

Variation 1. "If I ignore it, maybe it will go away."

The most common response to a partner's demand "Whose side are you on?" is withdrawal. A partner shrugs, leaves the room, or in some other way disengages from the conversation.

Divided loyalty can lead to panic: How can I choose between two people I love? How can I be a good son and a good husband? stuck between the "horns" of the dilemma, we cannot act. After all, the nature of a dilemma is that there is no clear or clean solution. Withdrawal may seem the best option.

Seeking His Response—and Driving Our Partner Away

Intense feelings are aroused when we experience the negative power of in-laws. We then seek resonance in our partner: "Do you understand what I'm feeling?" we demand. "Do you endorse or validate my feelings with empathy and concern?"

When a partner does not respond, we raise the pitch, hoping to get an engaged response if only we make enough noise. The principle is an old and tried one: If we cause enough fuss, we will get the attention we need. But sometimes, the more we raise the emotional temperature, the more others are likely to withdraw.

Luisa describes a furious quarrel with her husband, Eric, that occurred when she felt that her mother-in-law was particularly rude to her. "I shouted at him till I was blue in the face, but he

just froze and went for a drive. When he came back, he pre-
tended nothing had happened, so I started shouting again, and
he left again. When I try to talk to him about his mother, he
clams up, and either drinks a beer or goes to the pub."

Why do so many men ignore a wife's distress at in-law
problems?

Stonewalling, Stress, and Self-protection[1]

A familiar generalization is that men are more comfortable than
women in engaging directly in conflict. In a family setting, this
common "truth" turns out to be nonsense. In this setting, men
have a lower tolerance for probing conversation and verbal
conflict.

This is the surprising finding by John Gottman, who has
done long-term, meticulous research on married couples. One
element of his research involves a study of marital quarrels in
which the heart rate, blood pressure, and adrenaline levels are
measured during quarrels.[2] Gottman's studies show that in an
argument with a partner, a man becomes physiologically overwhelmed much more quickly than does a woman. A man's
pulse rate in an argument rises rapidly, along with his blood
pressure. Not only does his blood pressure rise more quickly
than his wife's, it will stay elevated longer. With his physiol-
ogy making him more vulnerable to stress, he may instinctively
remove himself from confrontation.

"Stonewalling"—the technique of shutting down recep-
tors and turning your body and mind into a stone wall—is
a defense against the stimuli that flood our system when we
sense danger. Going blank, refusing to show a response, or

leaving the room are all defensive acts. Withdrawal protects us from the discomfort of anger, and may protect others from our aggression.

In a state of heightened arousal, we face two options: We either fight or flee. Eric withdraws from Luisa to protect both of them. But to Luisa, withdrawing is a powerful act. It conveys disdain, icy anger, and rejection.

EXERCISES
to Engage a Partner Whose Help
You Need to Manage In-Law Conflict

When your partner is overwhelmed with feelings such as "There is no way of meeting her demands without betraying my mother or being a bad person," the challenge to a partner is to assure him, "You can help me improve the situation without being disloyal to your parents."

The first step is to move away from the position "It's all your mother's fault." To resolve the dilemma:

• Don't insist "You should support me and not your mother."
• Assure him that you value his bond to his mother, and you want to help him maintain it.
• Show your mother-in-law that you are helping her son sustain his bond with her.

This will have two positive effects: Your mother-in-law will be reassured that you are not asking her son to give her up; and she will be reminded that you, working together to show appreciation of her, are a couple.

• Get his attention without confronting him.

When an avoidant person is confronted, he shuts down and resists engaging with anything. Make sure he is not already in an anxious state when you try to engage him in discussion.

• Find a way to engage him positively.

Instead of saying "We have a problem" or even "We have to talk about this," choose a meal or an activity where you can also talk, so he can moderate his anxiety with distraction.

• Keep your messages simple and positive. You could suggest:

"When I feel uncomfortable with your mother, I'll reach out my hand for you. Will you take it? That's all you'll have to do to make me feel you're supporting me."

Or

"It would be helpful if you could say, at least once, in your mother's presence, 'I think my wife looks just fine as she is,' or offer some other compliment."

These are more effective requests than the global complaint "You never stand up for me."

• Translate very clearly what counts as "being on my side."

He may need to understand that saying something like "My wife is upset" or "This isn't the way I'd like you to talk to my wife" supports you without attacking anyone else.

Variation 2. Fixed position: "It's your place to show my mother respect."

The second strategy in dealing with a loyalty dilemma is to control the person who brings the dilemma to your attention. "Don't say anything bad about my mother" pushes the problem to one side. But it does not make the problem go away.

When Cal hears his brother's version of the quarrel that Shelly had with his mother, he says, "It's not your place to speak out to her." This "fixed position" technique is a simple way to avoid the loyalty dilemma. It closes the argument and avoids having to consider a partner's perspective. It is an avoidance strategy that turns the tables against anyone who makes a claim on you. "Whose side are you on?" is countered by "Whose side are *you* on?" The message is: "If you are going to be my partner, then you cannot ask me to question my parent."

The Explanation, and Remedial Action

Sometimes we are loyal to a parent because we feel guilty about our own critical views. We may silence our partner's criticism, just as we try to silence our own.

As a son contains what he thinks of as his own "disloyalty," he may be alarmed to hear his wife voice criticisms he himself wishes to suppress. Anxiously, he wonders: "What happens if I admit my own anger towards my parent?" and "Will I be able to contain it, once I acknowledge it?" Hidden away, denied open discussion, even small criticisms loom as large betrayals. The further down he buries them, the more unacceptable they seem.

EXERCISES
to Help Your Partner Support You

The ham-fisted order "Behave yourself!" is most effectively managed by responding to the positive, underlying message, which is "I need you to respect my loyalty to my mother."

- First, sidestep the attack, and respond to his vulnerability. You can assure him: "I want to join you in respecting your mother; I want to support your loyalty to her."
- Set out ground rules: "I want you to tell me when you are upset, but I cannot accept you shouting at me to silence me when I have a problem."
- Take preemptive action to assuage your partner's anxiety about rejecting his parents. Demonstrate to your mother-in-law that you do value her.
- Set out clearly what changes you want, and ask your partner's help in achieving these changes.
- Focus his attention by asking, "What is the alternative to supporting me?" Freezing you out with a fixed-position strategy will severely damage your relationship. If he understands the potential damage, change will make more sense.

Variation 3. "My parent's behavior is just normal behavior."

We expect a partner to share our views and our sense of what counts as normal. Two people in a couple may want and like very different things: One loves skiing, and the other hates snow; one likes theater, and the other is bored by it. But usually the two people in a couple share some sense of what's normal and what's bizarre.

Yet some norms are slow to reveal themselves. Our own family rules fade into the background of our minds. We take them for granted. We sometimes forget they are not universal. Our partner joins an overlapping family with an outsider's perspective. He may be amazed or even outraged by what we think of as normal. Our partner's different view of our family might seem like a betrayal: "How can you complain about what I consider normal?" or "How can you demand we change something that's inevitable?"

The third response to loyalty dilemmas is to refuse to consider your own family norms from your partner's perspective. "She doesn't mean anything by it" and "That's just how she is" and "You have no right to think there's something wrong with my mother" fix your position: "My family should not be criticized."

Whether this strategy is used as a gentle "I don't see the problem" or an accusatory "If you see a problem there's something wrong with you," it denies the legitimacy of a partner's perspective.

EXERCISES
to Broaden Your Partner's Perspective

Your aim is to persuade your partner to see things from your point of view without denying the legitimacy of his viewpoint. You can focus on your experience rather than on his family's flaws:

- Persist (gently but firmly) in telling him how you feel. Remind him how important it is that he understands you.
- If he complains that you are being wrong or unfair or mistaken in criticizing his family, respond to his discomfort about potential disloyalty, and remind him that you are focusing on your feelings, not his parents' flaws.
- Make a specific suggestion how things might improve. Assure him that he can help you change his family's behavior without being disloyal to them.

- If you are the one hearing criticism of your family, don't forget that your partner wants "resonance" in your response.
- While you may be hoping to keep an argument from escalating by appearing "flat" or "neutral", this nonresponse, from a partner's perspective, is frustrating.
- It is more effective to say how you feel ("I get upset when you criticize my mother").
- But also say, "I want to support you."
- Above all, avoid showing contempt for your partner's complaints.
- Remember, having different views is not a sign of disloyalty, but refusing to empathize with each other's view is disloyal.

Variation 4. "I can't deal with her but maybe you can."

Every marriage contains several contracts. Some of these contracts are explicit in the vows spoken at the marriage ceremony. Other contracts are implicit; sometimes we do not fully realize what a partner expects in a marriage. However, most people, in marrying, take mutual support as an essential part of marriage.

In some cases, an implicit contract may include the clause, "Help me deal with my family." This usually involves helping a partner fulfil their sense of duty to their parents. But sometimes it means, "Help me do the distancing work I haven't been able to do."

When your partner and your parent do not get on from the start, when they argue and engage in strategies of defiance, it is a reasonable guess that one of the qualities that attracted you is her ability to stand up to your parent. You may have a vested interest in keeping that conflict alive. A partner's hostility to your parent may help maintain the distance that you have been unable to negotiate yourself. When your partner does all this work for you, you may even be free to complain about her hostility, thereby feeling reassured about your underlying loyalty to your parents—while benefiting from the distance your partner achieves.

Boundary Lessons

It is often said that men are more comfortable than women in drawing strict personal boundaries between themselves and others. But this common belief about men and women has to be shunted aside if we are to understand why some men delegate borderwork to their spouse.

One reason the relationship between a daughter-in-law and her mother-in-law is problematic is that an adult son is less likely than his wife to have established skills and strategies for staking out boundaries between himself and his mother.

His wife is likely to have spent a significant part of her adolescence engaging in borderwork with her mother. *Borderwork* is behavior that reminds others, "I am not you. I am different from you. If you want to know who I am, you have to listen to me." Teenage girls are quick to stake out "identity reminders": "I haven't liked that since I was five!" and "Just because you do it that way doesn't mean that I have to!"

"You don't really know me" is a common theme in parent/teen quarrels. Teens work hard to shake a parent into a new awareness of who they are and who they want to become. The parrying that begins in adolescence never really comes to an

end; adult sons and daughters continue to be irritated, sometimes occasionally and sometimes regularly, by the parents' failure to keep their knowledge of a son or daughter up-to-date.

Though many adolescent boys (approximately one quarter)[3]
engage in identity-informing arguments with their mothers, the
majority of sons put far less energy into borderwork. Boys and
men are less comfortable in engaging in those interpersonal
arguments that fine-tune relational positions. While teenage
girls report having, on average, a fight every two and a half
days with a parent, and these quarrels last approximately fifteen
minutes, boys of the same age report having a fight once every
four days with a parent, and these quarrels tend to last only six
minutes.[4] Boys have less practice in giving parents lessons in
keeping their distance and acknowledging changing identities.

Moreover, sons have a ready-made assurance that they are
different from their mother. Few people assume that a son will
be "just like his mother," while many girls do feel the force of
that expectation. Whether the pressure is from cultural models
or other people's assumptions or from identification deep within
a girl herself, a daughter energetically engages—both positively
and negatively—with the assumption that she is "just like" her
mother. Sometimes a teen resists similarities through counterproductive, potentially self-destructive rebellion; but often borderwork achieves a positive, vital engagement. Her parents may
be slow learners, but she persists in teaching them about her
individuality until the relationship is altered and up-to-date.

By the time girls reach adulthood, they are women who are
likely to have gained experience in marking boundaries with their
mothers and fathers. At the same time, they have learned to reassure their parents that love and closeness remain alive, even as a

relationship changes. Boys, on the whole, have less practice and less finesse with negotiating boundaries while also offering reassurance. A husband may expect his wife to show more skill and persistence in reminding his parents of his adult identity and adult need for privacy.

But there is a catch. Your expectation that your wife will engage in borderwork with your parents may be hidden from everyone, including yourself. "I can't deal with my anger towards my mother, so I want you to do it for me" may be the unspoken deal. But when your partner goes to work, your response may be, "How dare you behave like that towards my parents!"

Yet even this dilemma has, in principle, a resolution. In the 2006 film *Monster-in-Law*, Jane Fonda plays an intrusive, demanding mother who contacts her son through a text or a call thirty times each day. The grown-up son never gets irritated, never complains about this daily interference. But his good-natured tolerance means that any wife will have a big job to do.

Beyond the simplistic portrayal of the perfectly bad mother-in-law and the perfectly good daughter-in-law, *Monster-in-Law* is a serious exploration of in-law interactions. In her role, Jane Fonda behaves as some in-laws do: She appears sweet, but delivers constant, indirect criticism of her daughter-in-law's social standing, her figure, her family. She appears welcoming, but tries to undermine her. In this fantasy tale, the prospective daughter-in-law is able to outwit her fiancé's mother, and negotiate a new relationship without involving the man who is both husband and son.

In real life, we need a partner's help in renegotiating in-law boundaries. Unilateral negotiation is rarely effective. But the realistic element in the film's resolution is that the improved contract includes both distance and inclusion. The daughter-in-law insists that her mother-in-law limit her daily contact, but she also insists that her mother-in-law spends holidays with them, and that she promises to be an active grandmother to their children. The clear message is: by accepting new boundaries around a couple, a parent-in-law gains a continuing relationship.

Deep Differences: Background

The story we want to tell about marriage involves two people who fall in love and decide to share their lives. We choose a partner for his individual qualities, but discover he brings with him a foreign inheritance. The closer a couple becomes, the more this inheritance can separate them. This inheritance includes a myriad of assumptions about family roles, about the meanings of day-to-day acts, about how to express love, care, and commitment. "Wait a minute," we protest, "these items were not declared on the premarital accounts!" He is amazed at our outrage, and declares his innocence: "I didn't hide anything." And when we look again, we see he's right. It's all there, in the background print of the family album.

We choose a partner who shares our interests and goals. We choose someone whose lifestyle seems to suit ours, whose conversational rhythms fit or inspire our own. We seek someone who matches our sense of the familiar. We look for someone who fits our sense of family. This should give our partner a head start at fitting in with our family.

However, there is another side to our choice of partner that actually increases the likelihood that the partner we choose will not mesh with our primary family. We tend to choose someone who offers something our own family lacks. We want someone who fills a gap in our lives. We want the warmth or the reserve, the security or the adventurousness, the decisiveness or the suggestibility, the humor or the seriousness that complements or compensates for our own family's repertoire of traits. This means that even when a partner seems to be a good fit, there are likely to be significant differences in underlying rules, habits, and norms.

While we sometimes challenge and defy these norms, our partner sees them as benign. He may feel he is betraying family loyalties if he takes our perspective. To prevent overlapping families from undermining a marriage, this notion of loyalty has to change.

OVERVIEW

One of the greatest difficulties in managing in-law conflict is dealing with the divided loyalties. When your spouse and parents quarrel, how can you support one while remaining loyal to the other? There are four familiar ways of trying to manage this dilemma, and these familiar strategies often make things worse:

- You avoid engaging with the problem, and hope that it will go away.
- You take a fixed and simple line, directing one to show respect to the other.
- You deny there is a problem, or any grounds for any complaint.

• You admit there is a problem, but feel that it's too much for you to manage, and ask your spouse to deal with it alone.

Each of these strategies leaves your spouse feeling unsupported and let down. As a result, in-law conflict leads to marital conflict.

EXERCISES
for Change

One of the strongest responses to in-law conflict is confusion: "My partner is my friend, my champion in other ways. He is sympathetic and responsive. Why isn't he on my side?"

Your partner may be deeply disturbed at the prospect of choosing between a spouse and a parent. This approach can be reframed so that change is achieved without anyone being forced to make such an impossible choice.

One of the most important things in instigating change is the ability to see that change is possible. This does not mean that we simply have a positive mental attitude. It means that we look at the problem and break it down into things that we can change.

We cannot, and should not want to, break the bonds of loyalty our partner has to his parents. These run deep, and are part of who he is and what he needs to be in his own mind: a good person.

But we can work with a partner to manage the power of those bonds. Resolving the dilemma involves getting your partner's attention, reducing physiological panic or "flooding," and supporting him when the fear of disloyalty arises. So,

- Assure him that you understand and appreciate how much he loves and honors his parents.
- Offer help in continuing and supporting the relationship with his parents.
- Explain that seeking respect from his parents is very different from rejecting his parents.
- Tell him over and over that in supporting you he is not being disloyal to his mother.

When you are the one being criticized for your loyalty to a parent:

- Respond to your partner's anger, but don't endorse criticism.
- Avoid criticizing your partner for her (or his) feelings.
- Focus on some specific things either you or your partner would like to change.
- Agree to negotiate (and enforce) that change together.

Behind the cry "Whose side are you on?" is a fear of exclusion and betrayal. When loyalty pulls are respected and negotiated, fear of betraying one's own family disappears. The dilemma "Whose side are you on?" can then be resolved by collaboration.

6. *What Is Happening to Me?*
Becoming a Mother-in-Law

THE DREAM of being embraced as a valued member of your new family is one starting point for in-law conflict. You hope your mother-in-law will appreciate all you bring into her son's life, and will be thrilled to embrace you as part of her family. You hope your daughter-in-law will respect what you, as a mother, have brought to your son's life. She will be eager to learn from you, and accept whatever you are willing to share. Talk will come easily, as will laughter. You expect that whatever is best in you will be duly appreciated.

The actual experience of being either a mother-in-law or daughter-in-law is often very different. Instead of stepping into a warm, welcoming embrace, you feel excluded and put under critical surveillance. Mothers-in-law confront the additional discomfort of that familiar, negative stereotype—the interfering, intrusive, generally obnoxious mother-in-law.

Becoming a mother-in-law is a significant transition in any woman's life. In my study most women approached it with goodwill; most women encountered difficulties; and most regretted that there was no general pool of knowledge to draw on for a positive model. A majority of the mothers-in-law in my study (thirty-three, or 68 percent) found the transition considerably more difficult than they had expected. Two women in one man's life share, at a profound level, many interests and aims, yet all too often they end up at odds, each feeling rebuffed or patronized by the other. Strategies commonly used to deal with these difficulties are often counterproductive. The more each tries to fix the relationship, the more uncomfortable both parent-in-law and child-in-law become.

Why do in-laws so frequently engage in these counterproductive strategies? Why, in effect, do the interpersonal repair strategies that generally work for us fail with in-laws? And what guidelines might be followed to produce the positive change we crave?

The Burden of Stereotypes

Male comic routines of the twentieth century have been criticized for perpetuating the negative stereotype of mother-in-law, but this role has been hedged with negative markers that are as old as the name. The Roman satirist Juvenal, in 100 CE, wrote, "Domestic accord is impossible as long as the mother-in-law lives." Under the entry of mother-in-law in the *Oxford English Dictionary*, a common usage of "mother-in-law" is shown to be a seventeenth-century reference to the "everlasting Din of Mothers-in-law." The eighteenth-century English novelist Henry Fielding observed, "The word mother-in-law has a terrible sound." In the nineteenth century, a comment in the *Daily Telegraph* proclaimed, "The drink of this name mother-in-law is composed of equal proportions of 'old' and 'bitter.' " In the twentieth century, Hillary Clinton used its negative force to explain the animosity towards her: "I apparently remind some people of their mother-in-law."[1]

Some stereotypes are so common, so embedded in a culture, that they can be effective even when no one mentions them. They have impact even when you are convinced that you reject the stereotype.[2] Negative stereotypes were mentioned by each and every mother-in-law in my study. The power of these stereotypes explains responses that would otherwise be dumbfounding. It condones irrational, hostile responses in people who are otherwise fair, and who in other contexts carefully check their biases against evidence.

Some women, as they find themselves moving into the role of mother-in-law, seem to enact the dark side of this image. Mona, on learning her son was intending to marry the woman standing before her, felt "a surge of hatred. I wanted to scratch her face, and poke my fingers in her eyes." Some women, as daughters-in-law, lock their mother-in-law in a negative schema, and see everything she does within that framework. Kim explains that she "just doesn't like" her mother-in-law, who "always gets her back up," but Kim is unable to explain further. "She annoys me. Everything she says sets me off, and I am always suspicious of her intentions. I just feel defensive and I can't get over that. When we're in the same room, it's like some fly is buzzing in my ear, and I just want to swat it away. I can't pay attention to what she says because I'm too involved in controlling my nerves. I don't really know why. She just sets me on edge."

In this chapter, we hear the voices of women who feel trapped by having this schema imposed on them, and we hear the voices of women who impose this schema on others. Each tries to behave well; but these efforts at good behavior constrict spontaneity and increase discomfort. As we hear their different experiences, and explore the context of their discomfort, we can work towards freeing everyone from this ugly stereotype.

Ruth, Joyce, and Peter: Shame, Guilt, and the Syndrome of Escalating Exclusion

Some daughters-in-law and mothers-in-law step easily into mutual friendship, appreciation, love, and loyalty. Sometimes a daughter-in-law is welcomed as the ideal daughter, and a mother-in-law is appreciated for the love and wisdom that informs her relationship with her son. "She's closer to me than my own daughter. I love her so much, I don't know how we could have lived all those years without her in our lives," reflected a woman in Estelle Phillips's unique study of women making the transition to mother-in-law.[3] Heather, who married Leslie at the age of twenty-nine, has found "an amazing mother-figure" in Tessa: "This is such a good part of my marriage. Tessa champions me in ways I just can't imagine my mother doing. She *gets* what I'm after, and what I'm up against. She has unquestioning belief in me. What a gift! What a perk of being married."

In the Bible, one of the great, classical declarations of love is made by Ruth to her mother-in-law, Naomi. "Where you go I will go, and where you stay I will stay. Your people will be my people . . ." The daughter-in-law's words proclaim her sense of belonging. Marriage is not just commitment to one person, but to an entire family, and the bond endures beyond a partner's death.

But a modern-day Ruth, a thirty-three-year-old lawyer, buries her face in her hands as she describes a recent visit from her in-laws: "Normally I'm a reasonable and fair person. Normally, I am quick to appreciate other people's qualities and to key in to their point of view. But these virtues fail to materialize in the presence of my mother-in-law."

Ruth highlights an uncomfortable truth: Ordinarily reasonable and fair people behave towards one another in less than reasonable and fair ways when they become in-laws.

The tension between Ruth and Joyce follows a common pattern: diffuse, penetrating, and apparently baseless dislike on a daughter-in-law's part, and a bewildered, increasingly angry reaction from a mother-in-law.

A cloud descends upon Ruth as her in-laws enter her home. The watchful presence of her mother-in-law disturbs the natural rhythms of thought, reflection, and relaxation she normally enjoys in her own home. Ruth becomes edgy, hypercritical, brusque, and reserved.

Joyce "watches" her daughter-in-law as she tries to make sense of Ruth's hostility. She "watches" in an attempt to understand the woman her son loves, and who finds her offensive. She has learned that her daughter-in-law will "take exception to everything" she says. She watches herself, too: "I can never just be myself. Heck, I don't know who I am with her. I set out wanting to be friends with her. I was willing to give it my best shot. But Ruth is sullen and cold. I pay her a compliment and she takes it as an insult. I ask a question, and she freezes, all offended. I try to watch what I say, but I don't have the slightest idea what she wants me to say."

Joyce is confounded by the split between her daughter-in-law's manner with other people, and how she acts in her presence: "I see her talking and laughing on the phone, and she's a different person. With me she's sour and withdrawn. What I want to know is, what kind of crime I committed for her to feel towards me as she does?"

Sources of Support in Becoming a Mother-in-Law

Normally when we feel wrong-footed by someone, we complain to a partner, a friend, or a companionable son or daughter. But seeking support within the family network increases conflict by triggering fears of divided loyalties. So, a new mother-in-law who genuinely wants to support her son's marriage has trouble finding a sympathetic ear. "If I bring this up with my son, he gets uncomfortable," Joyce explains. "However which way I broach it, it comes out as criticism, and I know that's not fair. My husband and I divorced a long time back, but we're friends, and I could talk to him, I guess. But he seems happy enough with Ruth, and who am I to mess with that? I have a wonderful lot of girlfriends, but this is something I'd rather not put on the table. Too easy for them to condemn her, but that's not what I want. Or I'd just look bitter, the typical mother-in-law. So I keep it to myself."

This is what many women do as they struggle with the transition to mother-in-law. They keep it to themselves. Some women are ashamed that they are not more successful in making friends with their daughter-in-law. They do not complain to their friends because they do not want to show disloyalty to their son and criticize the woman he chose. Many women believe they should keep this problem in the family; but in the family, they have no one to turn to.

With no source of comfort, with no positive strategy for change, a mother-in-law is in an emotional situation that is best described as being "cornered." When you are cornered, you have a limited number of options, none of which is satisfactory. You may opt for face-to-face pleasantries but vent your frustration in behind-the-back complaints. You may sulk, and hope that someone will notice and comfort you. You may decide to ignore your in-law, because there is no point in making an effort: You know you simply cannot please her. But shallow pleasantries and avoidance make matters worse. You can get out of a corner only by directly engaging the person who is boxing you in.

Mona, Kim, and Doug: Moving in Darkness

"I've tried a hundred times to show her I want to be her friend. Over and over again I say something nice, but I get nowhere. Ordinarily, I don't have trouble making friends. No one at work seems to find me annoying. I just don't know how to behave with her."

Like many women making the transition to mother-in-law, Mona resents the negative power of the mother-in-law image. "It's a trap. It's like Kim has permission to cold shoulder me and shut me out of my own son's life, just because I'm a mother-in-law."

At fifty-six, Mona has an active and youthful manner. She does not feel that she is too old to forge an easy friendship with someone Kim's age. "There's not the same generation gap that I felt with my mother-in-law. I get on fine with colleagues at work who are Kim's age. There's no barrier there. But with her—well, I'm like a blind person in some unfamiliar room. I keep bumping into things. I don't know why. I don't know what they are."

Like many women, Mona feels like a stranger in a foreign land when she interacts with her daughter-in-law. The most common word used by women to describe how they feel in a daughter-in-law's presence is "wary."[4] This wariness is far more than a passing awkwardness. Mona knows there is much at stake. "If I can't get past this, then what happens? Already I can see my son moving away. Her influence will grow, you know. That's how it is. Women have a real power over men. How simple is it for him to phone me? How easy is it for him to visit me? These are things she'll control. And there'll be all sorts of other things down the road, you know."

The stakes are high. You are desperate to maintain contact with a son or daughter. This spurs you to establish a good relationship with your son's or daughter's partner, to moderate any prejudice you might have, and to make compromises. But when you feel rebuffed and threatened, you become critical of the person who threatens you. An unfriendly daughter-in-law who cold-shoulders you appears less attractive, less warm, less suitable than your son's previous girlfriends, who, after all, did not threaten you in the same way.

A daughter-in-law wants to establish her place as the woman at the center of her family. She wants to secure a direct influence with her partner, and she may think her mother-in-law challenges those aims. In many overlapping families, positions are tested gracefully and gradually. Tension is transient, and negotiated with ease. But in some overlapping families, being

an in-law is like having to function as a blind person in an unfamiliar room. You bump against things and feel the bruising, but
cannot make sense of what has hit you.

Why Women's Intuition Sometimes
Increases In-Law Conflict

Most women pride themselves on their ability to "read" the people in their family. The special attention women give to domestic
politics—a skill referred to as "women's intuition"—maintains
family harmony. In the realm of in-laws, however, sensitive concern over the minutiae of domestic exchanges *promotes* hostility
as often as it promotes harmony.

The ordinary skills we have in reading the moods and motives
of people can vanish in a heartbeat. When our normal techniques for interpersonal connection and communication fail,
we lose our bearings. Gripped by fear of losing a relationship
we value, confusion and suspicion replace responsiveness and
empathy. We interpret and reinterpret what someone means by
what is said. Self-consciousness turns our usual deftness into
clumsiness.[5] We pick up signals, but decode them in ways that
seem bizarre to others. Sometimes our views harden; we justify
and overjustify our interpretation, and hold fast to our sense of
insult or outrage.

In becoming a mother-in-law, you can feel that your interpersonal skills have deserted you. Becoming a mother-in-law,
for many women, is like suddenly being struck with Asperger's
syndrome. Someone who suffers from Asperger's syndrome
has a limited social perspective, particularly in the capacity to
understand another's point of view, and to read social cues. One

common strategy for dealing with this limitation is to think in terms of general types rather than individuals. In some contexts, this can be helpful. If you cannot read this particular person, you can at least refer to general rules—for example, how to exchange greetings with different people in different cultures, and how to talk to a fellow student, and how to talk to a teacher. But when you refer to a simplistic and negative type, the interpersonal situation deteriorates.

When Mona does not understand Kim, she sees a "rejecting daughter-in-law." When Kim feels she is being misunderstood and undermined, she sees a "nasty mother-in-law." As each tries to deal with the other's unfairness, each draws on her own family's tool kit. But what we use to placate our children or our parents may have the opposite effect on our in-laws.

Different Behavior and Bad Behavior

When the family system we are used to does not function, we may try one thing after another, without being able to calculate the likely outcomes of anything we do. The language we hear seems similar to our own, but as we speak, we realize it is different. In becoming an in-law, we become an insider; we expect to find many similarities. But the more we get to know the overlapping family, the more differences we may discover.

It is difficult to identify, all at once, the differences between one family's rules and one's own. Differences remain hidden, for they lie on many different planes. Different families have different rules of behavior, and different scales of emotional expression, and different methods of controlling behavior.

How much emotion can be expressed, and for what purpose?

What volume of speech is normal? Is it acceptable to disagree with one another? How do people in this family signal approval or disapproval?

Using family rules and measures and control mechanisms, each of us comes to adjust our tolerance for noise, for mess, for outspokenness, for expressiveness, for disputes, for displays of affection. Shouting in some families is okay; in others it is terrifying—and has to be either punished or ignored. Some families accept open expressions of anger, unhappiness, or love; other families prefer a more moderate emotional climate.

Outsiders tend to see more of the superficial rules of a family's behavior. The underlying structures of family rules are revealed only through extensive contact. Even then, these may emerge gradually, piecemeal, and at random. This means that an outsider who is positioned as an insider can break a family's rules without being aware of any offense.

A myriad of reminders, encouragements, and punishments are exchanged daily in each family. A family's control system is regulated by pauses and silences, as well as with orders, warnings, judgments: "Don't swear!" or "What did you say?" or "That's nice language." Some families address infringement of rules with a sharp, loud reprimand. Some families work through silence. Some offer concern: one "isn't feeling well" or "isn't oneself today."

When we are not able to read these rules, we come to distrust the autopilot that regulates the give and take, the quick exchange of comfort and humor that characterizes good interpersonal communication. Instead, we either adhere to simple, strict rules of politeness (a strategy more likely to be used by a mother-in-law) or we spike our own behavior so that other people will be as uncomfortable reading us as we are reading them (a strategy more likely to be used by a daughter-in-law).

Handling Arguments

A great deal has been written about the clashes that arise from different styles of male and female conversations,[6] but the significant language gap between women of different generations, with different priorities and different alliances, has, very surprisingly, been ignored. In-laws trip one another up with underlying messages or projected meanings that can turn an apparently superficial conversation into a minefield.

Not knowing how to have a friendly conversation is discouraging. Inadvertently behaving badly, just because you don't know this family's rules, is frustrating. But not knowing how to argue with someone is devastating. Here you are, poised for self-defense, burning from an insult, determined to slam your point home, and either everything comes crashing down around you or you find you have made no impact at all.

Finding your way through an argument is as important as knowing how to be friendly. In-laws, however, tend to operate on the assumption that direct arguments are dangerous. Ruth discovers the dangers of direct confrontation the hard way: "About a year after we were married, I did actually confront her. We had a fight, and at first I thought it helped. But, ever since, there's been something else in her manner—a defiant coldness, like I proved just what a bad person I am. Now I feel even more of an outsider." We saw earlier how Shelly's attempt to defend herself with her mother-in-law leads her brother-in-law to confront her husband, and the quarrel spreads throughout the extended family. Yet some women find that their outbursts are ignored. Courage and determination can be useless if you don't know the rules of engagement.

Each family has its own rules for arguing, and part of learning how to be a family is learning how to argue. If you don't know how to argue, then direct engagement, with the consequent quick shifts in emotional temperature, is bewildering. Grace, for example, is confounded by the rhythm and rationale of her daughter-in-law's temper. "I feel I should take heed of that ad for *Jaws*," Grace tells me. "Just when you feel it's safe to go back to the water . . . Well, my daughter-in-law erupts over an 'issue,' and is as ferocious as a shark. Then everything is OK again—until the next time. But I never understand what sets her off. The whole time I have to watch my step with her."

The difficulty in navigating your way through an argument when you don't know the family rules, the anxiety of interacting with a person whose responses you cannot predict, can make us "play safe." This strategy results in a *good-behavior syndrome* that aims at avoiding conflict but ends up increasing discomfort.

The Good-Behavior Syndrome

In many couples, women's traditional roles in the home have been transformed; but a wife and mother still feel responsible for keeping the domestic peace, and may feel inadequate or let down when her efforts fail. On their own domestic turf, women may shout as often as men, and experience anger as men do; but they nonetheless are more likely to monitor domestic harmony. In the company of her in-laws, as each woman tries to demonstrate her value and worth, she may decide to give up on having her say, and opt for simply maintaining an *appearance* of harmony. Strict politeness then becomes the guiding theme of interaction, and each participant feels silenced. The shared aim of achieving a genuine connection is further thwarted.

The High Price of Good Behavior

The effort to avoid conflict strangles communication. Emma says that her mother-in-law's attempts to "get on" are stultifying. "All I get are routine niceties. The conversation might as well be pre-recorded. I get 'Oh, really?' and 'How lovely!' but nothing means anything because she's just being nice."

As mothers-in-law, women frequently describe a daughter-in-law as unfriendly or cold, and experience in her presence a bewildering, diffuse disapproval; women, as daughters-in-law, complain about blandness, superficiality, and insincerity.

Mothers-in-law may try to manage a daughter-in-law's unpredictable and diffuse disapproval by monitoring their own behavior, "walking on eggshells," and avoid causing any offense by being "nice" or neutral. They comply with the good-behavior syndrome to avoid conflict—particularly when they fear that such conflict will distance them further from their son. Such efforts, however, may lead a daughter-in-law to complain about unsatisfactory and empty conversations. Like a teen in hyper-irritation, a daughter-in-law may then want to emphasize her rough edges to show her mother-in-law that these controlled, limited, and shallow exchanges do not suit her.

In the grip of the good-behavior syndrome, we lose the ability for responsive, reflexive conversation. Emma says that, as a result of these "set pieces" and "routine niceties," she "gets on" with her mother-in-law, but at the same time says they have "a crummy relationship." A mother-in-law tries to avoid conflict by being nice; a daughter-in-law is offended by the superficial nature of their conversation.

One person tries to make things better, using strategies that, for the other person, just make things worse. Neither can learn from the other because, in the grip of the good-behavior syndrome, neither offers a clear explanation of her response. The good-behavior syndrome substitutes rigid forms of politeness for honest and open communication. When negative feelings rip through that curtain, the players have no practice in responding to and negotiating with each other. So, there is no buffer for their fury when it erupts.

The challenge is to learn how to speak out, with genuine self-expression, without setting off the alarms that lead straight back to silencing.

Making an Effort and Making Things Worse

In the "wary" in-law relationship, the learning curve in how to be with someone comes to a shuddering halt. Each knows something has gone wrong, but neither knows what, and therefore neither corrects it. Each tends to use the strategies she has been inclined to use in the past—but in this case, these make matters worse.

Clinging to a strategy in the hope of making matters better while your strategy is actually making matters worse is a downward spiral of interaction that is called *complementary schismogenesis*. The anthropologist Gregory Bateson describes this as "a mutually aggravating spiral by which each person's response to the other's behavior provokes more exaggerated forms of the divergent behavior."[7] The more Emma "bristles" at Sarah's "niceties," the more Sarah tries to avoid offense by sticking to anodyne rules of politeness. The more Grace tries to avoid her daughter-in-law's mood swings, the more uncomfortable and frustrated she becomes in the relationship she is trying to improve. The more Joyce tries to avoid giving offense, the more Ruth takes offense; the more offended Ruth becomes, the more meticulously Joyce follows her own rules of politeness. Each has different sensitivities and hypersensitivities, and those of each aggravate those of the other.

Good Behavior as Control

In the grip of the good-behavior syndrome, we put surface harmony above genuine communication. For a daughter-in-law who hopes to be appreciated for who she is and what she brings to the family, the good-behavior syndrome is at once disappointing and insulting.

Men in the family, with their lower tolerance in general for argument, are more tolerant of low-key, low-substance conversations. Keeping quiet during periods of family tension does not have any measurable affect on the health of men; but for women, refraining from speaking out, biting one's tongue, smiling when they are fuming, swallowing their complaints, have a marked negative impact on their physical and mental health.[8] Women are more likely to suffer stress from the silencing maneuvers involved in the good-behavior syndrome.[9] The good-behavior syndrome may keep the peace, but it does not promote well-being.

Good Behavior as a Disguise

The effort to control yourself, and to fit all behavior into the good-behavior mold, tempts people to make behind-the-back comments, engage in cold sarcasm, and disguise the jibes they cannot resist. We are naturally communicative creatures, and when direct expression is prohibited, indirect routes will be found. A common complaint about in-laws is that they are complimentary face-to-face, but engage in behind-the-back gossip. "To my face, my mother-in-law is sugar sweet and tells everyone she likes me more than her own children. But behind my back, she complains about my accent and my clothes," Jenny says. And many women complain about subliminal insults, such as being given a size "large" sweater by a mother-in-law who explains, "You probably didn't realize the ones you have are too tight."

These tactics take grown women back to the cauldron of schoolyard cliques. The men in the family are impervious to the cross fire, and simply do not see the battle being fought before their eyes. So, when someone feels she is being attacked indirectly, and she seeks support from her spouse, she may be told, "Nothing is happening" and "You're imagining things." Then the veneer of good behavior between in-laws leads to that familiar marital quarrel, "Whose side are you on?" That's the final catch in the good-behavior syndrome: It does not keep the peace.

Efforts to "get along" at the expense of genuine communication result in indirect aggression and self-silencing. These strategies do not tame the awful in-law stereotype. Instead, they leave it unexplored, and it becomes the proverbial elephant in the room, which people keep bumping into but never mention.

The Mother-in-Law's Unspoken Fear of a Daughter-in-Law

There are many cultural images that criticize and denigrate a mother-in-law. There is only one sympathetic exploration of a mother-in-law's primal fear of loss and displacement by a daughter-in-law. This occurs in a notebook that Maguerite Duras[10] kept in the 1940s. Her story, "The Stolen Pigeons," should be read widely as a tale that uncovers the unspoken terror of becoming a mother-in-law.

Duras begins with a sensitive description of a proud, older woman: Even in old age, when "the old Bousque woman" was "bent at the waist" and "barely taller than an artichoke plant," she walks nimbly, sure-footed, and her mind remains sharp, "filled with a pure form of curiosity." Her eyes are "intensely alive" in her old face; she shows a self-respecting kindness to others; and she inspires deference in others; in short, she represents the best of old age, the old age each of us hopes for.

This pride and vitality are undermined at every opportunity by her daughter-in-law, Jeanne. As the older woman becomes more frail, the younger woman's aggression intensifies. Each year, Jeanne's "tone with the old woman became sharper." She spreads gossip about how frail and unkempt the mother-in-law has become. Despite this, the villagers continue to love the old woman.

Eventually, however, the daughter-in-law succeeds in destroying her mother-in-law's standing. One night, inexplicably, the old woman sneaks into the family larder, and Jeanne discovers her secretly feasting on some pigeon pies stored there. Jeanne then spreads news throughout the village of this "theft." From that day on the older woman is so humiliated that she "didn't speak, nobody spoke to her either." She loses her intellectual curiosity, and becomes herself the object of others' curiosity. She experiences what today we would call accelerated death syndrome, becoming rapidly older, ash-gray and silent. She is afraid to move lest she set off the laughter that ridicules each of her actions. She takes "eight long months to die," but this delay only increases the delight the daughter-in-law "experienced when she could finally put all her mother-in-law's rags in a pile in the middle of the courtyard and light them on fire, a big fire than spread smoke through the whole village."

Marguerite Duras's disturbing story about a mother-in-law's deep-seated fears of being displaced and excluded by a daughter-in-law makes an original contribution to our understanding of the fears a mother-in-law has as a woman who will age as her daughter-in-law matures. While a dark image of the mother-in-law is familiar, this dark counterpart of a daughter-in-law image has not reached the cultural domain. Few women as mothers-in-law match the criteria of "monster-in-law," but the image of a mother who will not rest until she exhausts her resources in destroying her son's wife shadows every woman who becomes a mother-in-law. Duras is the first writer to have given definite form to the other side of this spectre, that of the mother-in-law's fear of being overtaken by caricature. But we can understand the one only if we also see the other.

OVERVIEW

In our own family, we learn how to be with other people: We see them respond, and come to understand them more. When we don't understand a response, we know how to prod them into a fuller explanation. We may even learn the essential trick of getting our own needs addressed without doing damage to the feelings of others. But with our in-laws, our interpersonal skills falter. Under pressure to "get along," genuine communication stagnates.

In this chapter I have presented a series of interlocking questions and problems that frequently arise in in-law relationships:

- Why do I feel so uneasy in her presence?
- Why don't the strategies that work well in other interpersonal contexts work in this one?
- Why do my efforts to be nice seem to make things worse?
- Why is it so difficult to argue?

EXERCISES
for Managing Conflicts without Reverting to the Good-Behavior Syndrome

All these problems can be resolved by breaking free from the good-behavior syndrome. This syndrome arises through efforts to control the awkwardness of in-law relationships, but in fact it reinforces discomfort and suspicion. There are nevertheless ways to break clear of this cycle. One secret to getting along with in-laws is learning how to avoid performing in public as the "good person" without reverting to the "bad, angry person" in private.

A mother-in-law can develop techniques for challenging the mother-in-law stereotype:

- Show respect for your daughter-in-law's individuality and boundaries.

    For example, acknowledge her territory and power, wait for the invitation to visit, and ask how long she is expecting you to stay.

- Celebrate her.

    Tell her what you like about her, think of ways she adds to the family resources, explain how her skills complement those of others in the family.

- Try to get to know her.

    Ask genuine follow-on questions about information she gives you: "What was the meeting about? What was the outcome?" as opposed to "Lovely!" and "Oh, really?"

    Use phrases signalling encouragement: "Go on," "Tell me more," and "I'm all ears."

- Show affection.

- Notice her.

    If she does not seem to be warming to what you are saying, and if she appears withdrawn, don't keep trying the same tactics. Give her some space, be patient, and try something else.

Both mother-in-law and daughter-in-law benefit by using the following tactics:

- Make a direct response to indirect criticism.

    For example, "It hurt my feelings when you said I looked heavier." In this way, we avoid an accusation about motive, but state how we experienced the remark. Find an opportunity to do this in private, but as soon as possible after the event, before selective memory sets in. You want to avoid the response, "What are you talking about? I never said that."

- Confront your in-law when her responses seem unfair and inappropriate.

For example: "I feel I've offended you, and I'm sorry." Avoid accusatory mind reading ("You're angry" or "You're sulking"). We have to be prepared to listen to an in-law's complaint. If we are shocked by what we hear, if we feel she is being outrageously unfair, we can step back and say, "That's not how I see my behavior, but I'll think about that."

- Watch the body language.

As in-laws interact with one another and talk about one another, they use telling body language that can enforce both the good-behavior syndrome and the avoidance syndrome. These "tells" include:

- false, fixed smile (corners of the mouth go up, but not eyes)
- false interest (eyes stare wide; and nods are routine, not in sync with conversation)
- shoulder judders—showing annoyance
- quick head shivers—like saying "yuck"

The first principles in freeing yourself from the good-behavior syndrome:

Don't

- say something only because you think it will please your mother-in-law (or daughter-in-law)
- put forth a lot of effort doing what you don't want to do and expect her to like you for what you've done

Do

- state your thoughts calmly, not aggressively
- repeat yourself, when necessary
- express regret when your in-law is upset, but don't blame yourself or your in-law

Help your partner develop skills in managing conflict.

- You can explain that you are upset by what his mother says; but avoid making a direct accusation against his mother along the lines, "She is cruel/insulting/mean."
- Remember what a difficult position he is in; he wants to be loyal to both of you.
- Behind-the-back criticism is a ruthless weapon, but you can coach your husband in defense tactics. His rebuttals to criticisms about you from anyone in his family should be gentle but firm; he can simply smile and shake his head, indicating his refusal to engage in such nonsense, or he can say quietly and firmly that he'd prefer not to listen to complaints about his wife.
- Show respect for his loyalty to his parents: Don't ask him to listen to global complaints about his parents' character or motives. Be specific about what bothers you. Whenever you want to change something, think about a positive and specific way to change it, and suggest ways to make that change.

Work with your in-laws to break free from the good-behavior syndrome.

- Invite criticism.

     When one of your in-laws seems upset, draw her out. You could ask, "I see you are upset. It would be helpful if you explained why." And then you have to listen, without putting up a defensive screen.

- Tell it as you see it.

     When someone says something hurtful, say so. "You may not have meant it this way, but this is how I respond to what you've said or done."

Ways to take care:

• Don't use a club to kill an accusation.

   When an in-law says you've done something wrong or inappropriate or unkind, avoid global dismissals such as "That's ridiculous" and "I never say that" and "Baloney."

• Remember that your own pain is not the final argument.

   It won't help matters to respond with pain or outrage, such as crying, or appeals along the lines "See what she says about me," or an attack on another family member with "Are you just going to sit there and let her say those things?"

• Work at distinguishing between what has been actually said and what meanings it has for you.

   When you feel put down or insulted, and you believe the insult was intentional, call her on it. Be direct about how you feel, and why; but do not accuse her of anything. For example, "What you've said hurts me. I feel that you are criticizing me."

• Avoid global accusations such as "You're always criticizing me" or "You're insulting me." Stick to the problem at hand, and try to solve that.

   You could even refine this with an appeal to her understanding: "I sometimes worry that my home is not as well organized as yours. But it would mean a lot to me if you realized I did my best."

Coda: A little bit married

An increasing number of couples form a partnership and share a home without marrying. These couples interact with one another's parents and siblings very much like married couples do. Without the defining ritual of ring and wedding, there is ambiguity about whether you are an in-law. Where, in such cases, is the sharp switch from easy acquaintance to suspicious intimacy that unsettles so many when they hear that first announcement of a son's or daughter's marriage? Where is the power play that so often is first experienced in the planning and funding of the wedding? And does a mother coach a cohabiting partner to be a "good wife" or "good husband" to her child?

The gradual, incremental steps many couples now take towards, or in place of, marriage pose new uncertainties for "nearly" in-laws. The state of being what Hannah Seligson calls "a little bit married"[11] allows a hesitant, awkward dance that mirrors those more concentrated moves of affinity and suspicion that we have found among in-laws.

The uneasy, often unspoken questions that shape relationships between a parent and the partner of a son or daughter who is "a little bit married" contain themes that arise from the primacy of parental concern:

"Why aren't you eager to marry her/him?"

"Are you looking around for something better?"

"How serious are you about her?"

"What's wrong with you that you cannot make a commitment?"

"What flaw in you is making my own child hesitant to marry you?"

The best way to get answers is by asking your own child.

Getting Used to Being an In-Law

The emotions of those who are "nearly" in-laws are usually less passionate and complex than those we have towards our in-laws. In the absence of a formal marriage bond, there is less threat to status, less intrusiveness, and less offense taken at minor slights. Parents who are parents-in-law may see a cohabiting couple as "not quite grown-up"; paradoxically, they are more respectful of boundaries. But after a time, strong feelings, whether of affection or hostility, creep in: "It's amazing how fond I get of her boyfriends," Maria says, "if they stick around long enough. There's that soap opera element: 'What is he doing now? What's happening in his life?' It's the kind of warm interest I've always had in her friends."

The affection has follow-on questions about practical involvement: what is appropriate, and what is not? For Maria the question is whether to give joint household presents to a couple who may not see themselves as a couple, or to try to contain her investment—both emotional and financial—in someone who may be "passing through" her daughter's life.

Parents' readiness to offer family-like affection is regulated, like a sensitive temperature gauge, to their own child's vulnerability. "What will my son or daughter suffer if this relationship ends?" a parent asks. Couples who are a little bit married, when very young, are often accepted as transient. When a son or daughter reaches the age the parents consider "just right" for marriage, there is anxiety as to the seriousness and potential commitment of that "almost" spouse. But when a nearly married couple are in their late thirties, the "almost in-law" relationship becomes low-key. By this time, parents have seen children's partners come and go. They have seen a daughter or son develop both personally and professionally, and the particular character of the in-law is less important.

In many cases, the state of being a nearly in-law provides a good opportunity to get to know the overlapping family, to ease in gently, and discover those family rules and norms that are often disguised by social rules of etiquette. It is a time during which the difficult dance steps can be tested, without there being so much at stake when there are missteps.

EXERCISES
for Almost In-Laws

The questions below can guide you through what may be a minefield, or a no-man's-land, or simply uncharted terrain when your son or daughter is a little bit married:

- Is your behavior consistent with your child marrying her partner tomorrow?

  Keep in mind that if you criticize an almost in-law today, your own son or daughter will remember this if they do marry.

- Is your behavior consistent with them breaking up tomorrow?

  Your son or daughter will be very upset by the breakup; it would be helpful if they did not have to deal with your extreme disappointment, too.

- Do you respect what your son or daughter tells you about their relationship?

  If your son or daughter says, "This is my life partner," then you are, in effect, a parent-in-law. As always, it is your child, not you, who decides whether you will have this role.

7. Is Any of This My Fault?
Hard Lessons for Ordinary People

THE COMPLEX power of in-laws is shaped by many things. First, it is shaped by the fear of losing a valuable relationship as it undergoes change. For a parent who becomes a parent-in-law, the fear is: "What will I have to give up when my child becomes someone's spouse?" For a new daughter or son-in-law, the fear is: "Will I be able to maintain an exclusive bond with my partner in spite of his or her love and loyalty to parents?" Next comes the shadow play of unconscious expectations as each in-law hopes to be embraced by the new overlapping family as the ideal parent or the ideal child: "Will my in-laws appreciate what I bring to their family?" and "Will my in-laws acknowledge what I give to my partner?" or "Will my new in-law appreciate how much I give as a parent?" These anxieties are underpinned by the evolutionary pull of our self-interested genes that would hoard all available resources for our own bloodline, and resist claims on those resources by in-laws, those nongenetic relations.

These underlying biases and insecurities, these half-acknowledged hopes and anxieties, are a staple of in-law dynamics. They make us uneasy about our own bad feelings towards in-laws, and they make us feel bad about ourselves.

How we think and how we behave in the grip of our negative feelings pose a challenge to our sense of who we are.

Generally, people see themselves as loving and caring towards family members. Yet, among in-laws, many people have a tendency to be less empathic, and less fair, than they are with their children, their partners, and their own parents. In the urgent guard we keep over our significant relationships, in the heated grip we keep on our family, in our need for special alliances with those we love, our normal balance of fairness and kindness can falter, and our breadth of empathy can narrow.

An essential and very difficult element in dealing with in-law problems involves understanding how we ourselves aggravate these special and strangely intimate relationships. The human mind has its own strategies, many that work below our conscious radar, for regulating mental pain. When we think that something we care about deeply is under threat, when we are stung by shame or regret at our own behavior, our mind works overtime to regulate the information it processes. In this chapter, I take a look at many of the ways the mind protects itself from the assault of unflattering information that disturbs our self-image as we engage with in-laws.

The Self-Protective Mind

The human mind is ingenious. It allows us to process and respond to information in our world; but it is also ingenious in its capacity to limit and control the information we process. The mind alerts us to the hard facts of our environment, so that we can respond appropriately. But the human mind also protects our feelings and our egos from hard facts, and makes us ill-equipped to respond appropriately to interpersonal situations that require critical self-reflection.

A lot of what we perceive and understand has an emotive content. In other words, we have strong feelings about what we know. These feelings include delight and interest and excitement. They also include anxiety and regret and guilt. Day to day, we experience a range of all these feelings. To manage the pinpricks caused by criticism and regret, the mind "automatically"—that is, without calling attention to its work—selects, transforms, or ignores information that arouses discomfort.

One area that we tend to feel passionate about is what can roughly be called our guilt or innocence. When someone criticizes us, when we fear that we have offended someone, when we act in ways that are not quite in keeping with our self-image, our mind springs to our defense. It shapes information to reduce its negative impact. We justify ourselves, and waylay the discomfort of self-reproach. "I can't believe this" and "I just can't take that in" are common responses to devastating, life-changing information. What is not always acknowledged is that these defense mechanisms also function low-key and day to day. The mind has a range of mechanisms for protecting our vanity.[1]

The mind's strategies for self-protection function smoothly and subtly. Such protection does not always help us when we want to resolve problems with other people. We need to understand others' perspectives, and we need to see the justice in others' complaints against us. Our outrage at someone else's behavior, our conviction that we ourselves are in the right, our passionately held memory of what we said or didn't say may be shaped more by defensive mental strategies than by acute and accurate perception.

The unconscious force of mental defenses may make resistance seem futile. However, we can override the selective and distorting autopilot that may protect our egos but that puts relationships at risk. We can do this by understanding what evasions we are prone to, and what blinkers snap into place when our ego is under threat. The strategies that sustain a comfortable self-image are neither inevitable nor intractable; if we catch these strategies in action, we can outwit them. Fairness, balance, and understanding of our just desserts may leave us looking into a harshly lit mirror, but this is a small price to pay for improving the quality of relationships that have such power in our lives.

In-Law Conflicts: Selective Memory

Memory is a valuable capacity. It allows us to reflect upon and understand the past, and to prepare for the future. But one way the mind may protect itself is by forgetting.

Memory of a traumatic event, for example, is so disruptive to ordinary thought and function that the mind protects itself by burying these memories away from day-to-day thoughts. The powerful negative emotions surrounding the experience remain active, even though the mind tries to process and tame them. On one level, then, it is as though the event were forgotten; on another level, it is as though this awful event continually recurs and is dealt with ceremonially, symbolically, sometimes through clinical symptoms. The aim of memory burial is to free us from pain; but its effect is simply to disguise what we continue to feel.

Self-protective strategies of remembering and forgetting can also be activated in more pedestrian ways, with much lower levels of pain. The mind wriggles away from unpleasant memories of things we did that we'd rather not admit to. Our memories of many details of an event may be crystal clear, while we forget the details that show us in a poor light. Memory can be an adept editor. Some of the worst in-law conflict arises over distorted and selected memories of uncomfortable interactions.

A Second Look at Familiar Conflicts

The best way to see how selective memory plays a role in in-law conflict is to return to case studies already presented and to consider how selective memory has shaped the stories each person tells of their own experiences.

Shelly's quarrel with her mother-in-law, Nora, arises from Shelly's attempts to explain how edged out she feels by Nora's inclusion of her husband's former wife.[2] Here, again, is Shelly's story:

> One day I thought I might just try to tell Nora how [having Cal's former wife at all family events] made me feel. My thought is: She gets her head round to my perspective, and we're sorted. So, I start telling Nora that maybe there's too much of wonderful Vera in the conversation, and that maybe Vera didn't have to be included in every family get-together. I knew as soon as I launched into my well-prepared speech that something was going real wrong. Nora went all stiff, and stared at me. I tell you, it was some stare! And then there was

some torrent of words I don't want to recall let alone speak out loud. I'm not a timid person, but that switchover to out-and-out rage made me feel sick enough to feel scared. The gist was that I was trying to split up the families, that I was a soul-destroying bitch, and such. I was tongue-tied and got out of her home, quick.

I told Cal what happened and he was real sweet. He saw the funny side of it, and the awful side. I was so relieved because at least he was on my side. Then Cal's brother came storming into our house, demanding to know why I had been attacking his mother, how it wasn't my place to speak out like that. Cal calmed his brother down, but then turned to me and said the same thing: "You don't show her dis-respect. You don't upset her like this."

The first thing to notice is what is absent from Shelly's story. She gives a vivid account of Nora's verbal attack on her, but omits any report of what she herself said. Nora, nevertheless, is stung by what Shelly says. In fact, Nora is so upset that she enlists her older son to confront Cal about his wife's behav-ior towards their mother. Shelly is confounded by the attack because she has no memory of what she might have said to arouse such outrage.

How We Filter Out the Role We Play in Conflict with Our In-Laws

In talking to people about their in-laws, I am continually struck by how often people describe in great detail what an in-law has said to offend them, and what slight the in-law had committed towards them. At the same time, I notice how often they leave out what they themselves said.

Self-defensive filters are put into place whenever we are under stress. "What did I say? I didn't say anything!" Shelly protests while Nora cries out against her daughter-in-law's "insults," and says "I get nothing but insults from her." The accusations and counteraccusations, the sincere claims to innocence and the genuine experience of being attacked, are common fodder to in-law conflict. As Dani Shapiro notes in her reflections on her mother's anger towards her in-laws, "It was as if she didn't understand that words have meaning and heft, that they would live on in the consciousness of the person at whom she hurled them."[3]

Putting to one side the question of whether Nora and her sons acted fairly or appropriately, Shelly's self-protective strategy prevents her from understanding how she herself might have contributed to her mother-in-law's anger. Her memory is selective in ways that absolve her of any responsibility for what's gone wrong. As she relates her version of events, her ordinarily observant mind blanks out the more unflattering explanations of this painful exchange. Shelly remembers all the awful things Nora said to her, but none of the (apparently) awful things she said to Nora.

The defensive filtering of unflattering memories may avoid immediate mental discomfort, but it impedes the quick-firing empathy that often resolves interpersonal conflicts as soon as they arise. "Oh, I'm sorry" and "I didn't mean . . ." depend upon our ability to see that we've done something to hurt someone. But Shelly does not see what she has done. She cannot recognize her mother-in-law's version of events because her selective memory does not match that of her mother-in-law. She cries out in all sincerity, "I didn't say that!" while Nora retorts, with matched sincerity, "Yes you did!" The conflict becomes further entrenched as each feels unfairly treated by the other.

When people describe in-law conflicts, either in the heat of expressive anger or in the brooding aftermath, their memories are vivid—but only for the slings and arrows sent by others. It is hard, exacting work to reproduce what we ourselves have said and done to contribute to the conflict.

Selective memory and self-enhancing memory are common defenses against discomfort, making us feel better but hampering remedies to interpersonal problems. When someone's behavior upsets us, particularly if we feel humiliated or rejected by it, we normally exercise the healthy option of blaming them for being unreasonable or unkind or ignorant. Memory often comes to our aid by fashioning past experiences to fit a flattering self-image. "Memory," writes Cordelia Fine in her book *A Mind of Its Own*, "is one of the ego's greatest allies."[4]

Disconnections

Some of the most frustrating in-law conflicts arise from a disconnection between how someone describes their behavior and what they actually do. In-laws are described as making assurances: "I would never disturb you" and "I wouldn't think of interfering" and "I'd never do anything to come between you." These words are spoken in all sincerity, while the person who utters them continues to disturb, interfere, and divide.

We saw Melissa's amazement when her mother-in-law made

no connection between her assurance of how she would behave and her actual behavior.[5] Melissa asks Ashley to give advance warning of when she wants Jon to visit, so that she and Jon can plan their weekends. Melissa asks Ashley not to phone after 9 p.m. so that they can relax together, uninterrupted. Ashley assures her, "I wouldn't dream of imposing on you" and "Of course, I want him to relax when he is home." At first, Melissa is soothed by this, but then discovers that Ashley's behavior does not change. When Melissa demands of Ashley why she is not abiding by the agreement not to disturb Jon late at night, Ashley is aghast: "I would never disturb him late at night." She drives a wedge between her description of what she does and Melissa's perception of what she does.

This specific type of disconnection allows us to declare ourselves, sincerely, to be accommodating, while remaining entirely unresponsive. So, when Melissa complains that Ashley is not keeping her word, Ashley is convinced that her daughter-in-law is being unfair. The disconnect in her own mind between what she says and what she does protects her from seeing what she is doing. This automatic defensive strategy caters both to our need to feel we are behaving well and to our reluctance to give up what we want to do.

Minimizing Reality

Minimizing is a specific kind of disconnection. It is a strategy for controlling the description of what you are doing, so that only the positive aspects appear. We saw how Abbey asks her mother-in-law, Donna, to space and pace her visits. Abbey explains that she needs her privacy, and time at home without visitors. Donna's response is: "I just want an opportunity to see my grandson."[6]

Donna focuses on her aim, which is innocent and reasonable. She is able to express her good motive with conviction because, in her view, only her good motives matter. She ignores everything else. She ignores the effect her behavior has on Abbey. She repeats her version ("I just want . . .") and casts aside any protest. Minimizing is a strategy that denies the validity of another person's emotional response. "You make a big deal out of everything" and "I didn't say anything: Why are you complaining?" and "I just want to visit; I'm not going to disturb you" are all examples of the minimizing strategy.

It may be convenient to control the meaning of your own actions, and make only the positive motives relevant; but refusing to focus on another person's negative experiences of your behavior has a high interpersonal cost.

Self-Justifying Criticism

If, in the shock of disappointment or distress, we do accept responsibility ("What a fool I was!" or "I shouldn't have said that" or "I understand why he was so mad at me"), the mind makes speedy adjustments to modify our self-critical view.[7] In self-protection, we not only edit a memory of what happened, we also reconfigure the offense: We may end up justifying our own bad behavior by exaggerating the offensive behavior of someone else.

We have seen self-justifying criticism in action in a number of overlapping families. Brisha freezes her daughter-in-law out of the "real family" portrait, and seeks to justify her behavior by continuing to list Jess's faults: It is more comfortable for Brisha to think Jess deserves this unkindness than it is to accept that she herself is being unfair. The common defense mechanism of exaggerating the faults of those people we treat badly further impairs the strange intimacy of in-law relationships.

Many of these deft, defensive steps play an important role in human resilience. They help us bounce back from daily blows to our self-esteem. It is much easier to shrug off a colleague's rudeness if I think it is all his fault, and do not worry what I might have done to spark it. It is much easier to maintain my confidence if I blame someone else's unreasonableness when I fail to make a friend. But sometimes it is necessary to put hard questions to ourselves: "How much of this is also my fault?"

Deflection

No one likes being criticized, and we are quick to defend our self-image; but criticism of someone we love also affronts us. So, another version of self-justifying criticism (strengthening your criticism of someone when you think you have been unkind or ungracious to them) involves deflecting blame from someone we love onto someone else. An in-law is sometimes blamed for behavior you do not like in your partner or your child. Lisa blames her mother-in-law for Andrew's inability to locate the butter in the refrigerator—a symbol, in her view, of his expectation that the women in the house will bring him what he needs.[8] Brisha blames Jess for her son Felipe's failure to be honest about their engagement. A parent may blame a son or daughter-in-law for their own child's lack of motivation, for his unhealthy lifestyle, or, for his excessive materialism. In that way, they protect themselves from being critical of someone they love, but this deflection of blame damages broader family relationships.

The technique of deflection puts the blame not where it belongs, but where it fits most comfortably. And it is more comfortable to blame an in-law for something we don't like in our child or our spouse. Amy Bloom, reflecting on her intense anger towards her in-laws, says, "Mostly, I am content to hate them. I can blame them for every quirk and bend I don't appreciate [in my partner]."[9] In-laws are convenient recipients of deflected anger. This allows us to feel angry without feeling angry towards someone we love. It allows us to blame someone else for our partner's faults. If deflection goes unquestioned, this defense increases in-law conflict without addressing the real problem.

Projection: Having Someone Else Do Our Thinking for Us

The mind's techniques for shaping and selecting information kick in whenever our natural levels of comforting vanity are under threat. They emerge at work when we feel badly treated by a colleague or a boss, and they emerge among friends when a complaint strikes us out of the blue; but in "that strange, strained forced intimacy"[10] of in-laws, they emerge with astounding regularity.

The term *projection* is based on the simple analogy of a device that projects an image contained in the device onto a wall or screen. In psychology, the term is used to describe the common process of projecting something that belongs inside us (and we don't like) onto someone else.

When people come to live under the same emotional skin,

as people within a family do, they sometimes project their own thoughts and wishes and fears onto one another. We share with family members a psychological intimacy, and see them as part of who we are. Sometimes we project our own wishes onto someone. "My daughter has always wanted to be a doctor," a mother may say, but she may be more accurately describing her own hopes. Sometimes we project thoughts and feelings we have but would rather not own. Projection allows us not only to believe that we do not have these thoughts, it also allows us to blame someone else for having them.

Perhaps projection is at work when Sammi bristles at what she presumes is her mother-in-law's criticism of her housekeeping skills.[11] Let's listen again to what she says:

> Visits from my in-laws pile on the stress. I try to play it cool, and say to myself, "They can just take me as I am." But as soon as Marge steps through the door I start seeing things that ordinarily don't bother me one bit. The homey feel in the living room suddenly looks like a train wreck. Marge is never outright critical, but last time she came she took that sorrowful look around the place and said, "You must be awfully busy at work." I damn near choked on that. What was she doing? Offering me some excuse for the messy house?

Sammi admits that Marge's behavior activates her own doubts: "It's all too easy to get that drill going, pressing on all those sore spots: Is my home downright unwholesome? Am I ruining my kid's life with this environment? Shouldn't—you know—shouldn't the sheets be smooth and straight? Marge doesn't have to say much to get that drill going."

Sammi blames her mother-in-law for measuring her against a

standard she wants to reject, but Sammi on some level embraces this standard. Her own anxiety as to whether she is harming her family by not fulfilling traditional roles comes into play. By attributing the criticism to her mother-in-law, Sammi buoys up her assurance that she resists these values and avoids having to confront her own ambivalence.

Sometimes projection takes the form of seeing someone else as feeling what you feel but would rather not admit to feeling. The frequent descriptions of a daughter-in-law as "cold" or "unwilling to be friends" may be an accurate description of a daughter-in-law's attitude; but the description may also arise from a parent-in-law's unwillingness to admit his or her own coldness. The "coldness" may, after all, be a result of two people interacting, each having some reservations about the other. The "coldness" complained about by the mother-in-law may not belong to the daughter-in-law alone.

Projection escalates conflict. It comes across as critical or accusatory mind reading: "You are cold" and "You are criticizing me." But projection is the exact opposite of real mind reading. Real mind reading involves empathy and understanding. We do not enter into another's perspective by projection; instead, we project some of our own, but disowned, thoughts onto someone else. The experience of being caught in someone else's projections is uncomfortable indeed.

Whose Image Are We Likely to Project?

The most common voice we hear inside our own head is that of a parent. This voice, heard over a long period of our development, has a habit of staying on and chiming in, unbidden. Its echoes represent, in part, what we ourselves think, and they partly interfere with our own thoughts. Sometimes it is difficult to distinguish between the different roles played by our mind's internal cast of characters.

A parent-in-law has the knack of slipping into our mind and taking on a parental role. The family structure makes it easy for the image of a parent-in-law to fit right over the mental template of parent. Sometimes this overlay strengthens the bond: A parent-in-law offers a family relationship that may complement what a parent offers, and fill in gaps in our need for care and connection. Sometimes our in-laws stand in for our parents in less good ways, and, as sometimes with our parents, we feel invaded by their words. Our mind seems intent on hearing their most blunt and biased turns of phrase and their infuriatingly familiar summaries of people and events. The ease with which a parent-in-law stands in a parent-like place in our psyche adds to the strange alchemy of in-laws.

Schemas: Mental Filing Systems

Schemas are like mental filing systems. They function partly as an ordinary, neutral concept and partly as a stereotype. A concept consists of general knowledge about how a generic thing—like a table or a cat—usually works and what it does. A stereotype is a rigid idea of how someone will behave and think. A schema has a looser, messier construction than a concept because it includes a wide range of associations, not all of which are activated every time we make use of it. A schema is more pliable than a stereotype, but it sometimes makes us behave as though we did embrace a stereotype.

Schemas influence our interpretation of what we see. We do not have to believe that a mother-in-law is bound to be awful for "mother-in-law" to awaken negative ideas.

A negative interpretation of a mother-in-law's behavior—as interfering, difficult, controlling, disapproving—slides smoothly and easily into the schema of mother-in-law. For example, ordinary ups and downs of interacting with a new acquaintance may be dismissed as initial awkwardness, or as part of the process of getting to know someone. If our responses are primed by negative associations, these initial interpersonal glitches are likely to rouse the "difficult" or "disapproving" associations. We respond to small difficulties as though they were big trouble—and so our negative expectations may play a self-fulfilling role.

A mother-in-law may see her daughter-in-law as disapproving, hostile, or edgy because in her mind, too, the negative associations stick to the mother-in-law schema. She anticipates, and therefore is quick to "see," rejection as she assumes the role of mother-in-law. Her attempts to avoid acting to type make her self-conscious and uncomfortable. This discomfort generates the communication problems that occur in the good-behavior syndrome.

Schemas allow us to process information efficiently. With their help, we rapidly extract key information and interpret it. Schemas help us streamline data from the complicated world around us. But sometimes "efficiency" leads to bias. If we allow ourselves to be primed by a schema, we may be caught in a loop. Positive information fails to register; we notice only what fits our negative expectations. We may be so transfixed by negative associations that we can barely see the individual person in front of us.

Schemas slip easily into stereotype; but we can nonetheless catch them out and challenge them. We can exercise our memories, and test our assumptions, and give our in-laws another chance, and so we can take on the challenge to be fair.

OVERVIEW

In brief, here are some of the strategies our mind uses to control information that unsettles our ego:

- selective memory—*remembering only those events that put you in a good light and put someone else in a bad light*
- self-justifying criticism—*strengthening your criticism of someone because you have behaved badly towards them*
- deflection—*blaming someone else (such as an in-law) for the faults you see in a partner (or child or parent) so that you can avoid feeling angry towards someone in your primary family*
- projection—*blaming another person for the beliefs, feelings, values, or motives that you yourself have but do not want to acknowledge in yourself*
- stereotyping—*filing our experiences in ready-made format, without assessing the accuracy of the associations that shape our interpretation*

In the thick of in-law conflict, these defensive strategies often work together, making it difficult to disentangle justified from unjustified responses.

Can We Resist Our Mind's Defenses?

The mind's tactics in regulating pain serve many good purposes. They make us more resilient. We are able to think well of our-

selves, move past disappointments or rejections, and move on
with our confidence intact. If we did not make use of defense
mechanisms, we would probably be clinically depressed.

Without the strategies that protect our egos, any interpersonal glitch would flood us with negative thoughts: "This is my
fault" and "I'm not good at this" or "I'm clumsy," "I'm stupid,"
or "I'm a bad person." This is precisely how someone suffering
from clinical depression responds.[12]

People whose egos are undefended are not merely less happy.
They are less good at solving ordinary problems than are people
who robustly (albeit sometimes unfairly) defend themselves.
They are more likely to suffer from heart disease, and less likely
to survive cancer; indeed, in general, they are more likely to die
early. A well-defended ego is good for our health.

But it is also necessary to manage the downside of our defenses.
While self-justification and selective memory and projection
enhance our self-image, they do not protect us from damage to
relationships. To protect relationships we need the courage to
shake off comfortable mental habits, and to see how we ourselves
contribute to the problems we tend to blame on others.

EXERCISES
for Reducing Your Own Bias in In-Law Conflicts

Just being aware of common defense mechanisms can make us
more reflective and more fair. Simple guidelines are

• Avoid (defensive) self-justification.
   This means that you get a grip on yourself when you find yourself saying or even thinking "It's not my fault; it's all your fault." Or

"I only did that because you made me angry/made me feel I wasn't valued/criticized me."

- Do not generalize from a particular action.

    "You always insult me" and "You always criticize me" are generalizations and should be avoided. It is more practical to consider the specific instance, and the immediate problem.

- Do not dredge up past events.

    "This is exactly the same thing that happened when we last visited" does not address the current problem. It is likely to lead to a secondary argument about what happened previously. Each person in the argument may draw on the defensive weapon of selective memory.

- Avoid character assassinations.

    "She never shows appreciation" or "She's always cold" or "She never lets me have my own special time with my grandchildren" may justify your anger but are unlikely to be accepted either by an in-law with whom you have a problem or by your partner. A good rule is to focus on what bothers you and why: "I feel hurt when she said that" or "I don't feel welcome in her home."

- Try reframing your complaint.

    Reframing entails putting a positive or sympathetic connotation on behavior that you experience as negative. Instead of seeing your in-law as "cold" or "critical," frame this behavior as that of a person on an emotional precipice. **Remember: the key to understanding in-law conflict is to trace the behavior that offends you back to a fundamental vulnerability.** The key questions are:

    "What is she afraid of losing?"

    And

    "What (status, power, relationship) is she trying to maintain?"

Having identified the vulnerability in the behavior, you can begin to address it.

- Show appreciation for what she brings to the family.
- Acknowledge her value to her/your partner.
- Express this with words, gifts, and time.
- Initiate expressions of appreciation (taking her out to dinner, cooking her dinner, taking her somewhere, offering to relieve her of a burden—from shopping to house painting).
- Don't make her feel bad if she is occasionally cross or critical.

Remember, we're likely to argue unconsciously to ourselves: *"If I was unkind, then the person I was mean to must deserve such treatment."* Self-justifying criticism makes conflict more difficult to resolve. Try to signal that your in-law has not behaved badly, and that you are not offended. Then, your in-law won't blame *you* for *her* bad behavior.

- Defy old schemas.

   Try to look at and respond with a new understanding of others' perspectives. Your in-law is not being "selfish" or "mean" or "difficult" but "worried about losing a special relationship" or "afraid of having her status undermined" or "trying to show she is making a valuable contribution to the home."

- Imagine something better.

   You have to be able to imagine how things might change if your behavior changes. This takes imagination and empathy—seeing things from another's point of view, which involves homing in on the other's vulnerability.

New Mind-sets

We sometimes need a new mind-set to tackle in-law problems.

Neither "This is all the other person's fault" nor "It's all my fault" is helpful.

Neither "It's the sort of thing that happens to me because I just don't know how to deal with interpersonal problems" nor "She doesn't know how to behave" is helpful.

Instead, we can view conflict as a problem that we can solve, and look closely for clues to a solution. Keeping in mind that in-law problems arise from complex interactions among several people, we can explore ways to change the systems.

The mind-set we need to manage the power of in-law conflict is shaped by the following thoughts:

- "I will look at myself from her point of view, take onboard what she has to say, see my role in the problem, and take steps to improve my behavior."[13]
- "Problems are inevitable, and they offer opportunities to learn about in-laws' expectations and family rules."
- "I will hear someone's criticisms and complaints, and I will address them. These may be unpleasant for me to hear, but not devastating to my self-image because I can change."
- "Seeing that I am at fault, too, doesn't mean I have to feel guilty, but it is a way of seeing how I have the power to get things right."

People who are able say "This problem arises from how we react to one another. I can change this" free their minds from bias. They become like good scientists who focus on a particular problem and see the evidence before them, rather than like clever lawyers who use their intelligence to plead a specific case. The aim is to look at a problem without worrying about "Who is right?" or "Who is to blame?" The question is: "How can I help solve this problem?"

8. *Who's the Mother Now?*

Becoming a Mother, Becoming a Grandmother

WHEN Chrisy's son was born, her appreciation of extended families deepened. "My mother used to say, 'You won't appreciate me until you have children of your own.' I hated hearing that, over and over. But now I know what she means. There's this connection that you never want to break. It's overwhelming, because you'd do anything for your child. And I'll feel the same about his children. I get it now, how important the bloodline is."

Bringing a new child into the family is probably the most powerful of all human experiences. The transition to parenthood makes an immediate emotional impact; the experience is, as Chrisy remarks, overwhelming. Alongside the primitive wonder of birth is the presence of a new human being, packed with his own responses and interacting intensively with the world around him. The scientific basis of family continuity is no longer attributed, literally, to "blood" but to chromosomal inheritance; yet the psychological pull of "one's own flesh and blood" remains as strong as ever.

In becoming a mother herself, Chrisy discovers that "connection you never want to break," and this changes her relationship with her own mother. There is a new closeness with her mother, whose familiar sayings and habits no longer rattle her. The transition to motherhood changes and strengthens her relationship with her own mother.

Becoming a Mother Makes You Feel Closer to Your Own Mother

Many women experience a new closeness to their mothers when they themselves become a parent. They enjoy a mother's new pride in a daughter who becomes a mother herself. A daughter's past irritations and complaints are often counteracted by a mother's support, help, and delight. Many women are chuffed by their new status as mothers, and feel they have gained some kind of parity with their own mother.

This new closeness is not always comfortable for a woman's partner. When Chrisy's parents come to stay for a month following the caesarean delivery of their son, her husband, Tony, grumbles that, "They take over the house. They give our builders instructions. They add to the list of jobs we've already negotiated. Next thing, they reorganize the entire house. I found them washing the car yesterday, and now, as you can see, they're working on the windows. They create this *bustle* everywhere, and are pleased by all the good they think they're doing." He then smiles, wiping out the grumble. "But Chrisy needs her mom now, and I'm out all day, and in the evening I just concentrate on my son."

A son-in-law's ability to avoid interaction with in-laws moderates the tension. Tony can opt to be away from home, or be otherwise engaged when he is at home. This disengagement provides the "re-grouping" time we all need to maintain our mental equilibrium. Usually, we gain this from the comfortable "off stage" privacy of our domestic lives; but in-law visits interrupt the restful flow of reflection. Chrisy explains:

> At first, my mother-in-law's meddling was only mildly irritating, but now it drives me wild. She tries to take over my baby when she visits. She's like a vulture. She grabs him away and barely breathes a "hello" to me. She gives this running commentary: "You need to burp him; this is the best way to do it"; "He must be teething, you don't need to feed him." Then, when I want to let him play on the floor a bit, she hassles me about feeding him. When I tell her how he should be put to bed—no blankets—she nods, but doesn't pay any attention. I find some blanket she's unearthed somewhere all around him. I know she loves him, but I'm his mother. Except when she's around, I just feel like one mass of irritation. There's not one part of the house she doesn't barge into when she's here.

The birth of a child who is also a grandchild gives mother-in-law and daughter-in-law a new shared focus, but sometimes this shared focus rips in-laws apart. Chrisy feels at once invaded and ignored by her mother-in-law, Jean. The "help" and "advice" interfere with Chrisy's intensive new mother learning about what her baby wants and needs, how he will respond to being held, being put down, being tired, being ill.

Sometimes, too, Chrisy thinks Jean is taking over as the mother in the house. She feels that Jean is showing off her expertise at Chrisy's expense. Their shared focus on her son is neither comforting nor supportive. Instead, Chrisy finds much of it intrusive, critical, and competitive.

The Grandmother's Perspective

For Jean, the birth of her grandson is an opportunity to show her real appreciation of Chrisy, and to extend their relationship. "We've had some hiccoughs in the past, but here's this new link. I really hoped we could make a fresh start."

Instead, Jean finds her daughter-in-law more guarded, more short-tempered, and less tolerant. "No matter how hard I try to be a help and not a burden when I visit, I can see she thinks I get in her way. But I'm not going to give up my grandson. He's growing so quickly. I want to be a part of his life. He's such a delight. He's wound himself right around my heart. If Chrisy doesn't like me, that's too bad. I'll see this child I adore every chance I get."

The terror of being barred from her grandchild, the desire to witness and participate in the child's development, are every bit as strong in a grandparent as they are in a parent who is denied access through divorce; but the grandparent's voice has rarely been heard and rarely given due respect.[1]

Many grandparents are taken aback by the power of their attachment to a grandchild. They are also taken aback by the need to negotiate their access with an in-law. The ups and downs with a daughter-in-law then take on a new urgency.

Becoming a Mother Drives a Wedge Between Daughter and Mother-in-Law

Some years ago Lucy Rose Fischer looked at the ways a woman's relationship with her mother shifted when she herself became a mother.[2] She found that the birth of a child has a clear impact on the mother/daughter bond: There is more mutual, active involvement; there is renewed closeness and less strain and greater appreciation of company, advice, and support.

Another question then intrigued Fischer: "How does the transition to motherhood affect a woman's relationship with her mother-in-law?" She found that this transition also increases the interaction between mother-in-law and daughter-in-law, but instead of reducing strain, it increases conflict. The boundaries a daughter-in-law has established suddenly became ambiguous. Sharing a child with a mother-in-law forces a new, not always welcome, intimacy. Even women who generally have a good relationship with their mother-in-law can feel extreme irritation with her after the birth of a child. Among in-laws, new connections do not always bring new closeness.

Decoding Irritation

Sometimes it is difficult to give any rational explanation for the irritation we feel. Irritation is a primitive response, familiar from childhood. Though most people gain greater control over their irritability, and do not stomp and scream as a child does, irritability does not become more subtle and layered as people mature. Our expressions of love, hatred, jealousy, and admiration may become more sophisticated, but irritability feels as primitive when we are thirty as it did when we were three.

Nevertheless, irritation signals something deeply wrong in our environment. We say people are "just annoying"; but sometimes our so-called "irrational" irritation is fine tuned and intelligent when we put it in context.

Becoming a mother is an exciting and rewarding experience,

but it also threatens a woman's grasp on her identity. "Will I still be me if I have a child, if I become a mother?" "Will I lose my particularity, my priorities, my acuity?" "Will I simply be an instrument for my child?" Suddenly, and piecemeal, difficulties in pursuing your own interests and goals cascade into your daily life. "Where is the person I used to be?" a new mother asks. In the context of these questions, the heft of a mother-in-law's intense focus on a grandchild throbs like a toothache.

Chrisy and Jean have a child and grandchild in common. Sharing a child invites more interaction, more mutual involvement, and more claims on each other's time and space, and each is more vulnerable to the other's demands.

Jean's running commentaries on the baby's needs distract Chrisy, and disturb the rhythm of her own thoughts. After the birth of a child, a mother engages in an intensive learning process. How should the baby's movements and cries be interpreted? What is the best way to soothe him? What helps, and what hinders, his feeding? Jean's comments interrupt Chrisy's own learning process.

Another trigger of annoyance is the undercurrent of competition over maternal expertise. Chrisy sees Jean as touting her own knowledge at the expense of her daughter-in-law.

New Connections, New Boundary Tensions

Chrisy's complaint that her mother-in-law is now "all over" her son, that she "swoops down on us with new force" signals a common tension. Following the birth of a child, it becomes more difficult to regulate boundaries between the two generations.

The powerful attachment grandparents have to their grand-

children can override the deference they previously showed
to a couple's privacy and independence. When a grandchild is
born, most of us are eager to participate in the first few weeks
of the baby's life. Some women hope to stay with the couple,
and enjoy the day-to-day contact as they help with the endless
tasks of baby care. One woman lobbied her son to be given the
opportunity to be present at the child's birth, a wish shaped by
love and delight, but also an impossibly intrusive request. Even
a grandmother who, in other contexts, meticulously respects a
daughter-in-law's wishes may resist boundaries set on her access
to a grandchild.

The strategies that mothers-in-law used included minimization and coercion. Minimization, as we have seen, involves
controlling the description of what is being done in ways that
make any objection seem disproportionate: "I'm only coming
for a short visit" and "I just want to see my grandchild" or "You
won't notice me. I'm just coming to help out."

They frame their requests in miniature, and paint over
objections. "You're not going to keep me from seeing my own
grandchild, are you?" or "You're not going to deprive him of his
grandma," they plead, and dismiss a daughter-in-law's need for
peace and privacy. If a new mother insists on marking boundaries, the tension escalates.

How Setting Boundaries Can Escalate Demands

A child's mother is normally the gatekeeper to relatives. A
mother-in-law's fear and resentment may appear disproportionate, but register unease at a daughter-in-law's power. At the

same time, a new mother, as daughter-in-law, needs new kinds
of privacy and assurance, and may be more sensitive to others'
control.

A negative cycle occurs: A daughter-in-law emphasizes the
boundaries between her and her mother-in-law; a mother-
in-law's fear of exclusion is activated. Will she be deprived of
her own child and grandchild? Seeking reassurance, she may
defy the limits that her daughter-in-law sets. In response,
the daughter-in-law doubles her efforts to mark boundaries, and this in turn increases a mother-in-law's anxiety about
disconnection.

In some cases, in-law tensions evaporate with the birth of a
child. Becoming a mother, after all, secures a daughter-in-law's
status; she is now the mother in a family of her own. In the
early years of their marriage, Rosa could barely believe she was
lucky enough to have James as a husband. She competed with
her mother-in-law for "first of kin" status:

> I used to flaunt my special relationship with him. I reminded
> her, every chance I got, that I was the most important woman
> in his life. I'd throw in little bits of information when we
> talked, just to show her how much he was mine and not
> hers. I'd mention little habits—what he did when he woke
> up, and how he had this special yawn and stretch. I'd always
> refer to me and him as "we," and wonder if she noticed what
> message I was sending.
>
> When we had our first child, I realized I didn't have
> to force this point: my gorgeous son and I were definitely
> James's primary family. Now I look at her and think, "How
> did you put up with me?" It's like coming out of adolescence,
> and feeling bad about the hard time you gave your mother.

While there are no universal patterns of response in in-law chemistry, each mix contains the enduring questions: "How close am I to the people I love?" and "Do I have my family's respect?" These shape both in-law conflict and its resolution.

Irritation and Self-Doubt

The question "How well am I caring for my child?" is always a heated one. A new mother faces overwhelming pressure to deal with minute-to-minute particularities of parenting; at the same time she is under pressure to demonstrate to others and assure herself that she is a "good mother." A good mother is someone who is able to read her child's needs from his cries, coos, and fussing, and who responds appropriately. Someone who "helps" a mother may be heard as implying "I know how to be a mother, and you don't."

Anxiety and Competition about Motherhood

In recent decades, the question "What is a good mother?" has become more pressing, and the answers have become more exacting. More parents have responsibilities both in the workplace and in the home, and, in consequence, have less time to devote to child care. At the same time, the quality of parenting is constantly assessed. Children are seen to need educational stimulation from birth onwards. They are required to have enrichment through art, sports, music, and language. In addition, they require emotional support to sustain them in a complex society. Parenting is judged not just for adequacy but for excellence. It is also competitive, since no one wants to fail one's child by being less than the best parent possible.

The changes from one generation to the other, in parenting styles and expectations, lead to different assessments of good child care. While the myth of the nuclear family proclaims that these clashes are irrelevant, that it is the parents alone who should have control and care of their children, the emotional and practical realities are very different.

Passionate Care; Passionate Disagreement

The love of a new child gives a woman and her mother-in-law a common focus, and it also presents new points of conflict. While grandparents today provide crucial child care, social changes lead to clashes between women of two generations who negotiate work and parenting in different ways.

The "mommy wars" between mothers who are in paid employment and mothers who work as full-time mothers are normally waged by women of the same cohort. Each woman feels that the value of what she does, and her style of parenting, is undermined by the preferences of the other. But different preferences and parenting styles also spark conflict between mother-in-law and daughter-in-law.

Anxiety about meeting the current standards of good parent, and anger towards anyone who—either directly or implicitly—questions another's lifestyle, is likely to trigger a hostile defense. One accuses the other of being selfish and allocating more time to career and income than to her children; the other lobs back accusations of her own—the "stay at home mother" is lazy, overdependent, and uninteresting.

How can a grandmother stand respectfully aside when she thinks the mother of her grandchildren is not the best possible parent? "The best thing for my grandchildren is for their mother to stay at home with them," says Chloe, Denise's mother-in-law. "I know that's not fashionable. I know that's not Denise. But that's what I want." Denise's mother, Alicia, is also concerned at her daughter's workload. Alicia shares many of Chloe's views about child care and family stress; but nonetheless, for Alicia, her daughter comes first, and she gives priority to Denise's needs. Chloe's priority is with her own immediate kin.

The heat of the "mommy wars" is stoked by uncertainty: "Am I doing the right thing by my family when I spend so much time at work" versus "Am I wasting my professional potential by spending so much time with my children?" Contemporary parenting ideals are so exacting that no parent can fulfil them. Every parent's choices and necessities defy at least some ideals, so any challenge ignites anxiety.

On more mundane, day-to-day matters, too, the question "What's best for the children?" lays a minefield between mother-in-law and daughter-in-law. Jean thinks that Chrisy spoils her child by giving him what she calls "redundant and extravagant" toys, whereas Chrisy thinks Jean spoils him by allowing him snacks whenever he demands them. Lois is uncomfortable with the strict religious upbringing that Laura is (in Lois's view) "foisting" on her children. Lois worries, "She is taking these children further and further away from me. I can't participate in this religious fervor." Chloe thinks that Denise is forcing her daughter to grow up in "an academic hothouse," whereas Denise thinks that Chloe undermines her attempts to prepare her for a competitive and demanding future.

Many conflicts signal generational shifts in child-raising norms, but they also frame an enduring competition between two women in their maternal roles. A grandmother may be eager to show how good she is at mothering—still hoping, perhaps, for a daughter-in-law's appreciation of her maternal value. A new mother wants to demonstrate her own competence.

"Who is the mother in the house?" casts down the gauntlet as a new mother lays claim to maternal authority. Competition escalates as each act of child care is framed by "Which mother knows best?"

From a mother-in-law's point of view, her valuable experience should be put to use; but a daughter-in-law may consider such experience outdated and short-sighted. And while most mothers-in-law say in all sincerity that they simply want the opportunity to participate in a grandchild's life, that they do respect the mother's child-rearing preferences, they also have strong views about what is best for their grandchildren. The love that brings the women together also puts them at odds.

The Importance of Resolution

If I had considered only this one aspect of in-law relationships, I would have seen the importance of improving these difficult relationships. Negotiating the trips and switches of overlapping families so that parents and grandparents alike can fulfil their legacies of care is an essential skill. There are no easy solutions when so much is at stake. The balance between a grandmother's emotional involvement and the modern assumption that a mother has primary control is difficult to achieve, but the cost to many generations of not finding such a balance is high.

There is the gamut of unnecessary suffering from the daughter-in-law who says, "My mother-in-law has made my life a misery. She tries to control everything I do because I'm the mother of her grandson," to the mother-in-law who asks, "What have I done to deserve this ban against seeing my grandchildren. Look at me! Do you see the evil woman my daughter-in-law sees? The one who isn't fit to have contact with the boys who matter more to her than anything in the world? How can she break my heart like this?" This needless suffering lays waste to the possible benefits to children of contact with grandparents, and the emotional and practical contributions that grandparents might make to the entire family. The cost of this conflict is high indeed.

The Evolutionary Importance of Grandparents

A grandmother's participation in child rearing has ancient roots and serves an evolutionary purpose.[3] Human communities became stable only when women lived long enough to be grandparents. They were then able to provide additional care for children. These first grandmothers could pass on accumulated parenting knowledge, and assist in the difficult task of providing food. In ancient societies, those parents who had a parent still living were more likely to see their children survive to adulthood. These ancient roles have a legacy in contemporary emotions.

Modern grandparents continue to provide a range of support. They assist their children financially, sometimes by offering direct assistance and sometimes by taking on child-care tasks. By allocating their time to child care, grandparents free up the couple's time to develop their careers. The term "human capital" refers to workplace skills, dexterity, and judgment that are attractive to employers and economically productive. A grandparent's offer of child care, then, can add to her own child's human capital, and improve the lifetime earnings of the couple. While grandparents may not play the role they did in ancient societies, social changes in parents' employment actually increase the potential input of grandparents today.

The strength of the extended family is clear and present, in spite of frequently repeated remarks about the decline of the family. When Michael Young began exploring the nature of the contemporary family, he found a simple way to assess the reality of the extended family. He scanned school records throughout Britain to see who the "just in case parent" was—that is, the person who would be called upon to care for a child if the parents were not available. In overwhelming numbers, the "backup" carer was a grandparent. In one primary school in London, with 243 children from different families, as many as 181, about 75 percent, gave grandparents as their emergency contacts.[4] This suggests that three-quarters of the children had regular contact with a grandparent, and that parents recognized grandparents as a reliable source of care.

The practical help provided by grandparents is increasing. Grandmothers now are a staple in the portfolio of child-care provision across all classes, across all ethnic groups. When both parents work, the support of grandparents is a boon to both child and parent. In single-parent families, a grandparent can provide a lifeline. The Grandparents Association has found that in the United Kingdom, 60 percent of child-care provision is provided by grandparents, and one in every hundred children is living with a grandparent.[5] The inability to include in-laws and to collaborate with them, and to negotiate comfortable boundaries, would have a high cost for everyone.

OVERVIEW

In-law relationships flourish or founder on what can loosely be called a relational system regulated by the following three questions:

"How can each assure the other that responsiveness to the other's needs and expectations of the extended family will not involve more loss than gain?"

"How can each use her own initiative to celebrate the other's contribution to the family, without being coerced by each and every expectation and wish?"

"Will your claims undermine my need for attachment and respect?"

Each demands that the other accommodate her. But without a flexible mind-set, neither will improve the interactional system.

EXERCISES
for Change Involve

- Identify specific behavior you want to change
  Remember: The thought "She is incapable of change and this situation will not get better" is almost always wrong.
- Identify your own role in the situation you want to change
  Remember: The thought "This is all her fault" is almost always wrong.

• Identify a positive outcome

Remember: You will be more effective in improving a situation if you concentrate on the positives ("I would welcome visits like this, interactions like this") than if you concentrate only on the negatives ("I don't want visits, and I don't like these conversations").

EXERCISES
for a Mother-in-Law

Many issues that underlie in-law conflict are deeply embedded in assumptions and insecurities of which we are only half aware. A lot of background work, in the form of reflection and introspection, has to be done before anyone can begin to improve the relationship. We are then better placed to identify specific problems and to consider appropriate strategies for change.

• Think what you'd like to say to your daughter-in-law about her parenting practices.

Saying this aloud to yourself might help you catch things that would be unacceptable to her.

• Accept that your views of parenting may differ from those of your daughter-in-law.

So, what do you do? Do you convey your frustration and sense that your expertise is being rejected? Or do you show her you are willing to learn from her?

• Remember that when you give advice about raising a child, your daughter-in-law may hear it differently.

She may hear you saying, "I want your child for myself," "You don't know how to raise children," or "I don't trust you."

• Find ways to assure her you accept her parenting styles.

You can admire the way the baby responds to her. Tell her how

well she managed something. "He's happy now," you could comment when she picks him up.

EXERCISES
for a Daughter-in-Law

A new mother is justified in putting her and her baby's needs
first. At the same time, a grandparent's attachment is likely to
add a great deal to a child's life, and it makes sense to shape this
into a family-friendly form rather than fight it.

- The template "I'm the parent, and you have no rights over this
  child" deprives your child as well as your parent-in-law of a
  potentially valuable relationship.
- Many fierce battles arise as a mother-in-law's fear of exclusion
  is aroused. Therefore, think of ways to be proactive in offering
  reassurance of connection.
- Think of ways to celebrate what a grandparent can offer a
  child.
- Show your mother-in-law that your child benefits from her.
- Consider how you can protect your own domestic privacy while
  allowing a grandparent access to a grandchild.
- When you find yourself engaged in those "cognitive loops" in
  which an in-law's irritating behavior is visualized over and over
  again, ask yourself, "What is the benefit of holding on to my
  anger?" Then reflect, "What can be changed?"

EXERCISES
for Working Together

Many of the conflicts described here appear between mother-in-
law and daughter-in-law. But they are always triangular: They

may appear to be just between two women, but these conflicts are crucially affected by a son's willingness (or resistance) to do maintenance work himself.

- Can he ensure that his parents are comfortable with inevitable shifts in the kinship networks?

  He can keep in touch with them, keep them up-to-date with personal news, and show his appreciation of them, so that his parents can be assured that their relationship with him will continue, even as the bond to his wife intensifies.

- Is he helping his parents feel connected to their grand-children?

  He can provide a route to special communication between his child and his parents, so that his parents do not feel dependent only on a daughter-in-law for access to their grandchildren. The more active he is as a father, the more reassured his parents can be.

- Does he present his wife as *his* authority on child care?

  In that way, he will persuade his parents to respect her as well.

- Do you both show appreciation for his parents as grand-parents?

  Husband and wife can work together to celebrate the grand-parents' contribution to the family. If husband and wife take the lead in shaping and regulating the grandparents' contributions, the power of in-laws is more likely to have a positive effect.

9.   *What Do I Owe You?*

Gifts and Debts; Love and Gratitude

"**LOVE** and money don't mix" and "It's just business; it's not personal" are familiar sayings that make no sense within the emotionally charged context of family life. In families, everything is personal. The exchange of money and gifts between family members is usually framed as a sign of love; in consequence, complications in those exchanges drive questions about how much, how equal, and how trusting is that love.

Parents often express some of their positive feelings—love, support, faith—by giving help of various kinds. Help is an expression of connection. Families offer a network that supports its members through commonplace ups and downs of fortune. With financial loans, gifts, or investments, they cushion the aftershocks of ordinary upsets. When a business fails or illness strikes or unemployment makes new career training necessary, a family can provide a safety net, and limit the impact of a misfortune. For the most part, financial help is provided with goodwill, and received with gratitude. For the most part, expectations are clear, reasonable, and flexible.

But sometimes things go wrong. Gifts change their meaning as feelings change. Generosity gives way to resentment that someone is taking advantage of you, manipulating you, or misusing your gift. Among in-laws, unease about generosity, reciprocity, and gratitude is less easily negotiated than among blood relatives, and it is more likely to escalate. Conflict over gifts and debts blurs their financial borders and floods our emotional territories with an unstoppable, bitter force.

A History of Money, Marriage, and In-Laws

Marriage, money, and in-laws are intricately linked in many societies, both ancient and modern. The word "wedding" comes from "wed," which was the symbolic payment made in early England by the bridegroom and his relatives to the wife's family. In many African societies, marriage involves a series of "prestations," or payments, gifts, and services, made by the husband and his family to the wife's family. Throughout a marriage, ritual exchanges of valuables—similar to birthday or Christmas presents—mark and maintain friendly relations between the two separate families that are joined through marriage.[1]

The "wed," the payment to the wife's family, was made in acknowledgment of the family's loss of a daughter upon her marriage. It compensated her parents for the cost of raising a wife for their family. The wed is very different from a dowry, which is offered to the husband and his family by the wife's family. From Classical to Victorian times, a dowry was exchanged as a means of giving a daughter her inheritance when she left her own kin, and it was also a means of securing status within her new family.

Dowries transfer wealth from the bride's family to the husband's, and this gives the bride's family the incentive to be

choosey about a son-in-law. Dowry practices and arranged
marriages go hand in hand so that a family that gives away its
wealth on marriage has some say in who receives it.

The Terrifying Face of Contemporary Dowries

Neither the wed nor a dowry, in their traditional practices, is
fairly construed as buying a wife or selling a daughter. The
exchange of goods, gifts, and services carries symbolic meaning. These exchanges mark the mutual investment two families
have in the couple and their offspring. In some contemporary
practices of dowry exchange, however, the coldness of financial
assessment joins up with the dark forces of in-law relationships.
In defiance of current antidowry laws, some families in India,
Pakistan, and Bangladesh have transformed the ritual dowry
practice into one modelled on buying and selling products at a
specific cash price. The "price" of a husband rises with educational qualifications. Doctors, chartered accountants, and engi-
neers demand a high dowry from a wife's family in payment for
their status. Payment is due in cash, and agrarian families may
have difficulty raising the cash demanded.

When the "price" is not paid, the worst possible in-law scenarios can be enacted. Isolated, without power in her husband's
family, a daughter-in-law may suffer a range of abuse. Sometimes this abuse becomes violent; sometimes it becomes deadly.
When a husband's family does not receive the expected dowry,
or when a wife's family falls into arrears with dowry payments,
the debt may be discharged through the daughter's death. There
are about 6,000 "dowry deaths" each year in India alone.[2] Since
so many of these deaths involve burning and are disguised

as kitchen accidents, they are referred to as "bride burning." The dowry practice that once protected a daughter when she became a daughter-in-law now reduces her to a commodity.[3] These extreme cases offer a harsh reminder of the potential destructiveness of in-law conflict.

Remnants of Old Practices

In the United States and in Britain, where the families in my studies about in-laws reside, marriage is no longer seen primarily as an alliance between two families. It is seen as an alliance between two individual people who themselves chose each other on the basis of individual compatibility. Even so, there are clear relics of old practices in current customs. The exchange of rings between husband and wife reflects the old practice of ring exchanges between the two sets of parents-in-law. The customs of the father "giving away the bride," and of the wife's family paying for the wedding celebration, are remnants of the dowry.

Though only these few modified relics remain, a marriage bond still involves mutual investment of two families. Parents and parents-in-law alike have a stake in the couple and their offspring. The exchange of material goods, gifts, and services between generations of interlinked families is still significant, both symbolically and emotionally. Familiar gripes—"She never thought I was good enough for him" and "They never thought he was equal to her family"—echo the myriad ways in which a partner is assessed.

"What does he bring to your family?" and "What does he offer your child?" and "Does he raise, or does he lower, the

overall status of your family?" are questions inextricably linked
to questions about who is gaining more from the marriage, and
who is giving more, and who owes what to whom.

The Dangers of Giving; the Dangers of Receiving

Bonds to your own family are expressed in day-to-day acts of
giving and receiving. While family members exchange gifts and
mutual care because they want to, because the well-being of
other family members is bound up in their own, they also have
expectations of some exchange, in terms of gratitude, compli-
ance, or reciprocity.

Giving—whether it is time, care, or money—has many
motives. There are the motives we acknowledge: "I want you to
be happy" or "I want you to be comfortable." There are motives
that people are likely to deny: "I wanted you to be in my debt"
or "I want control over you." There are motives that may come
to light only as we experience disappointment or regret and
realize, "That's why I did it!" or, perhaps, "What a fool I was to
expect that!" There are also motives that others impute to us
("You just want to patronize me" and "You want to throw your
weight around"), the unfairness of which may take our breath
away, and yet may have a grain of truth.

Among members of our own family, a passionate concern for
one another's well-being usually controls resentment or fear or
regret when exchanges of gifts go wrong. But even among our
blood family, disappointed expectations of what we will gain
by giving form part of the deep cultural register. The story of
King Lear can be seen as a morality tale about the possible consequences of generosity to one's own children, the disappointed

expectations of gratitude, and the loss of control when you give away all you have. Quarrels among siblings over family inheritance are common, as each sibling clamors for material proof of a parent's special love. But among in-laws, where mismatched expectations abound, gifts of a material nature are more likely to generate confusion, offense, and hostility.

In this chapter I consider three common patterns wherein financial matters lead to in-law meltdown. In the first pattern, the mutability of a financial exchange leads to confusion and a sense of betrayal: "It's not a gift, it's a loan, and you are now in debt to me." In the second, generosity can set precedents, and expectations escalate: "My in-law will take everything I have" or "My partner is not able to deny any request my in-law makes." In the third pattern, a so-called gift comes with obligations and control: "I did this for you, so you have to do what I say." So, the offer to pay for a wedding or a vacation may come with strings: "I'm paying, so I get to organize every last detail." A contribution to education or to a business enterprise, too, can have an undeclared interest: "I gave this to you and meant for you to use it *my* way." Apparent generosity is then followed by accusation: "You wasted my gift" and "You are unworthy of what I have given you."

Carrie, Stephen, and Clare: Financial Flash Points in Families

The intense conflicts over finances that arise among in-laws center on common in-law themes: "Do you appreciate what I am bringing to the family?" and "Are you willing to show me the respect I deserve?" Some psychologists who specialize in in-law relationships have seen so much conflict over even minor financial exchanges that they advise issuing a written contract with every financial transaction.[4] Unfortunately, no written contract would sort out the divided feelings and the push-pull between husband, wife, and parent-in-law that are enacted within financial exchanges.

Carrie and Stephen were married when Stephen was a senior in college. Stephen's mother, Clare, said she would pay off her daughter-in-law's student loan as their wedding present. As the couple chose an apartment, they factored this gift into their budget. Soon after they moved, however, Clare explained that her business had taken a downturn, and she was no longer in a position to repay the student loan. Stephen accepted this, but Carrie protested: "Absolutely not! We had an agreement."

No formal contract would resolve this conflict: Stephen does not want his mother to feel financial hardship, whether or not she made a clear commitment to repay his wife's loan. He argues that he and Carrie are young, that at their stage of life debt is manageable, and, in any case, he does not want to argue with his mother over this.

Carrie sees the matter differently. She remains focused on the principle of sticking to a promise. She and Stephen made decisions based on that promise. She accuses Stephen of being afraid to confront his mother for rescinding this "gift." Her husband seems more protective of his mother than of his wife, and Carrie feels betrayed. Stephen argues that he is right to be protective of his mother, and he is hurt that Carrie is willing to be so harsh, so punitive towards her. Isn't one of the roles of a wife to help him honor his parents?

Arguments, Resolutions, and Meltdown

As Stephen and Carrie argue, their differences become entrenched. Stephen says it is no big deal; most of his friends are paying back loans. Carrie insists that is not the point. His mother made a promise. Stephen casts doubt onto whether this was a promise as much as a statement of good intention. "Her business got into trouble. That happens. I don't want her to have to take out an expensive loan to pay this for you."

Stephen begins to explain the differential interest rate between a loan that his mother would have to take out, and the rate of interest that Carrie pays on a student loan. Carrie becomes impatient and interrupts. She reminds him that Clare has just bought herself a new sofa and had her house repainted, and that there is no sign that *she* is cutting back. She also reminds her husband that Clare has bought them an expensive table for their kitchen. Stephen says this is a sign of his mother's generosity. Carrie says, "No, it is a sign that she can afford to pay off the loan—which she promised to do—and isn't doing."

As they argue, each marks a position in an opposing camp. Stephen thinks they should be generous towards the mother, and worries that Carrie is being "stingy" in insisting that his mother repay the loan. Carrie thinks her mother-in-law is stingy to decline to pay off the loan. In-law tension over finances turns into marital strife.

Separating the Elements

Carrie and Stephen are engaging in their own highly individual argument, but the themes they grapple with are common in many arguments about in-laws and finances. These four elements are

• *misaligned protectiveness*

Protectiveness is key in family relationships. It is a central feature in both marriage and parenthood. What is less widely recognized is how often children reciprocate by feeling protective of their parents. While protectiveness normally cements relationships, among in-laws it can get caught in the cross fire.

• *isolation*

When we are hurt and insulted, we seek comfort in a response that is often called "validation." This simply means we need someone else whose opinion we care about to see things from our perspective, and to agree that we have been treated badly. We need reassurance that such treatment was undeserved; we need to share our complaint; but most of all we simply need someone to say, "Yes, the way you see this makes sense." Without this support, we feel utterly isolated.

• *betrayal*

The heated question here is "Whose side are you on?" Each feels the other is taking someone else's side: "Why are you siding with your mother rather than me?" and "When you attack my mother, I feel you are attacking me."

• *bewilderment*

In the grip of financial problems, a host of questions emerges: "How did this gift suddenly turn sour?" and "Why is this offer of 'help' so much trouble?" Flooded with confusion, we sometimes forget to ask practical questions; yet practical questions alone can guide us. We need to take a deep breath, shift from emotional to pragmatic gear, and ask, "Given we have this problem, what should we do now?"

Misaligned protectiveness, isolation, betrayal, and bewilderment pack in-law and marital tension with explosives. The only way to diffuse the tension is to identify and contain different flash points. When the issues are out in the open, neither sees themself as "totally right" and the other as "totally wrong." The two opposed people can form a couple again and move forward, each supporting the other.

Harriet, Adam, and Danielle: Children Supporting Parents

In some societies, gifts and payments between in-laws are strictly regulated according to customs. Today, in the United States and Europe, there is very little social protocol to guide expectations or regulate appropriate gratitude and reciprocity. One couple may be clear about what to expect from their family, and what is expected of them in return; but each person within a couple may have a very different view about family obligation. Under the influence of those selfish genes, our thoughts may be less generous towards an in-law than toward a blood relative or partner. We have a habit of giving more weight to the needs of our primary family than to the needs of others. These different measures can cause in-law conflict and move on to cause marital conflict.

Adam's mother and father were divorced when he was twelve, and his mother, Danielle, provided for him and his sister while

they were going through their turbulent teens. Now, at forty-
five, Adam has established a modest but consistently successful
business and has, for many years, been able to provide for his
mother. His wife, Harriet, also contributes to the family income,
and she assesses the high cost of the college education looming
ahead for their two children. Her sense of obligation therefore
is adjusted by the needs of her children:

> I don't begrudge Danielle a place to live and decent clothes,
> but her extravagances bother me. I think we should control
> some of her spending, if it's our money. But when I say this
> to Adam, he gets red in the face, and goes on about the sac-
> rifices his mother made for him, and that I don't understand
> how families work. I know he thinks I'm mean, and there is
> no way I can get through to him what my worries are.

Familiar interlinked elements of in-law conflict emerge:

• misaligned protectiveness

Adam is protective of his mother, and feels that Harriet is
attacking her. Harriet is protective of their children, and feels
that Adam is failing to look out for their best interests.

• isolation

Each refuses to see the other's perspective; each sees the
other as failing to understand the situation. Adam says that
Harriet does not understand how families work. Harriet says
that Adam does not understand how families work. Neither
feels "validated" by the other—that is, recognized, confirmed,
supported. Each gets a negative, blocking response from the
other.

- betrayal

Adam feels unsupported in his family duties by Harriet; Harriet feels that Adam is neglecting his duties to their children. Each feels betrayed by the other's lack of support.

- bewilderment

"How did this happen to us?" and "What is really going on?" are questions that stir up anxiety and even rage. The step forward is for Adam and Harriet to join forces and ask, "How can we solve this problem together?"

A couple do not have to see eye-to-eye to support each other; they simply need to acknowledge the legitimacy of the other's view. Entrenched right or wrong positions must be modified. Harriet is not a mean and selfish person denying her mother-in-law support; she focuses primarily on her children's financial needs.

If the framework is revised, then a real discussion, and not simply a clash, can ensue. Questions can be reshaped so that they can be approached jointly: What can we do now? Can we limit what we give Danielle? Can we set aside more college funds from some other source? Can Adam explain to Harriet how their children's college costs might be met at the same time he helps his mother? Can Adam and Harriet together identify what they will need for themselves and their children? Can Harriet be clearly informed as to what funds go to Danielle?

No one other than Adam and Harriet can provide a satisfactory resolution to their conflict; but to achieve this, each needs to participate in the financial decision, and each needs to have a say in the allocation of their funds.

Social Changes and Changing In-Law Conflicts

Small social changes cause big shifts in family life. Over the past two and half decades, patterns of education and employment have delayed the age at which a young person can expect to be "a real grown-up," in the sense of being financially independent.[5] Many people, now in midlife, reflect that when they reached adulthood, their parents believed that financial support from parents should stop. "You have to stand on your own two feet" and "Independence is the key to success" and "If I keep helping you out you won't grow up." Parents who continued, at that time, to support their adult children were thought to "spoil" them. Besides, the only people who did this were the rich people who, it was sometimes said, had more money than sense. Today, however, even families with a very small discretionary income offer crucial emotional, practical, and financial support to their adult children.

Investments in a young couple's future often yield high returns. Whether you support their education or offer them child-care time or provide a place to live in your home, such support enhances their chances of accumulating human capital—that is, the skills, experience, and knowledge that facilitate careers. Since the career of your son-in-law or daughter-in-law also benefits your own child, "investment" in your in-laws can benefit the people you care about most.

When Andy and Lewis married, Andy's parents consoled themselves about Lewis's minimum-wage job on the grounds that he had potential. He spoke about going to community college to obtain a business qualification. They then learned that Lewis's parents refused to fund the tuition for the course.

Lewis's father said, "He's over twenty-one. He's on his own. He should take care of himself."

Andy's parents did not agree. "Parents should help launch their kids, if they can, as long as their kids are willing to work for it. Lewis is only twenty-two. That's not fully grown up in our books. It's cruel not to make this easier for him."

Andy's parents decided that they would fund Lewis's tuition. Andy's mother, Meg, explained, "What's good for him is good for our daughter. She chose him, and we weren't thrilled, but we have to accept her choice. If he can better himself, then it's better for her, too. So we'll pay the tuition. I see it as a good investment."

When Lewis lost interest in college after one semester, he was surprised by his parents-in-law's accusations that he was wasting their money and he would have to pay them back.

The expectations of what was given and what was expected were out of sync. Lewis understood the financial help as a gift. Meg and Max, however, were making an investment on behalf of Andy, who would be the long-term beneficiary of her husband's education. Lewis demands, "Am I supposed to let them run my life, just because they're paying for this course?" Each player in this financial arrangement has a very different view of its meaning, and each feels unsupported, let down, and confused.

Is There Any Way to Separate the Emotional from the Financial Issues?

Disappointment and conflict in the wake of financial exchanges between in-laws is such a common pattern that Gloria Call Horsley, a therapist with expertise in in-law conflict, declares unequivocally that every financial transaction between in-laws should undergo a due diligence examination and be subject to an enforceable contract.[6]

A contract has the possible advantage of cutting through selective memory: What did I say when I offered the money? Did I say it was a gift or a loan? What were the expectations when I accepted the money, either as a gift, a loan, or an investment?

But a contract will not address the deep tensions that arise. While clarity may prevent bewilderment as a "gift" becomes an "investment" or a "loan," misaligned protectiveness and a sense of isolation and betrayal inevitably follow when the agreement falls apart. However, a couple's mutual protectiveness can make any financial difficulty bearable.

Niall's father, Frank, offered to help the couple buy a house soon after they were married. With the cost of a home many times higher than even a good salary for a young adult couple, their only opportunity to buy a place of their own was with parental support. Niall and Ella were delighted to have Frank's support.

Then, five years later, Frank declared that he needed the capital he had put into the house, and asked Niall to "buy him out of his share of the house." During those five years, the value of the house had increased considerably. To agree to his request, Niall and his wife, Ella, had to sell the house to have enough funds to recompense Niall's parents fairly.

Sometimes financial help is a poisoned chalice. Both Ella and Niall feel insulted by this unexpected claim on what had been perceived as a gift. "We could have called his bluff," Ella explains, "and said, 'This was a gift.' We could have demanded proof of anything else. We actually went as far as to consult a lawyer on this. But to go further . . . Well, that sort of thing can mess up a family, totally. Frank is our children's granddad. Niall and I talked it through. We decided that his father was being really thoughtless. But we didn't want to turn it into a family battle. We didn't want the children to see us having this kind of battle with their grandparents. Niall was so mad, so hurt, I told him that the best thing was just to sell the house, and find something we could afford, all by ourselves. This isn't so bad. This isn't a tragedy. But it's been a hard decision, and hard to stick to—the decision that this is not going to be a big thing in our lives, or even a big thing between us and Frank."

Niall experiences his father's demand for the return of a "gift" as a personal rejection. Ella buffers Niall's pain by emphathizing with it, and also ensuring that the conflict between him and his father does not escalate. Neither feels betrayed by the other, because their protectiveness is aligned. Neither is isolated because each has the other's support. Sharing the problem and focussing on a solution utterly transform a potential in-law war into a manageable disappointment.

OVERVIEW

The conflict that arises from financial issues between in-laws is never just about money. It involves questions about love and understanding and gratitude and resentment. Addressing key questions can lower the risk of escalating anger and accusation, and help realign protectiveness:

- Who is protecting whom?
- Does your partner feel rejected by the way his or her parents are dealing with the financial issue?

- Does your partner feel protective of his or her parents?
- Are you able to see a partner's vulnerability and respond to it even if you do not share it?

If you are able to consolidate a protective alignment and acknowledge your partner's perspective, then neither feels utterly alone. Neither will feel marginalized or betrayed.

EXERCISES
to Do Before Accepting or Offering Financial Gifts

Gifts and reciprocity, gifts and obligation have ramifications beyond finance. They link up with genuine care, with the wish to help and participate in others' lives. Sometimes they also link up with a desire for power and control. Many problems arise from a misunderstood or unacknowledged agenda. Mismatched expectations about the meaning and purpose of the gift, the loan, or the investment are at the root of most in-law conflict over finances. Here are questions to pose to yourself before you enter into any financial arrangement with in-laws:

- How grateful do I expect my in-law to be for this gift?
- What do I expect my in-law to do with this gift?
- What are other possible outcomes, and how will I respond to them? How can I make this clear to my in-law? (If I do, will the gift still be acceptable?)
- How will I feel if I give my in-law something, and then find that my in-law (or the couple) cancels a visit or declines an invitation to dinner or a request for help?
- If this would offend me more after I have been generous, then I should either refrain from giving anything, or revise my expectations.

Remember: In your primary family, expectations for giving and receiving have probably been absorbed into the family culture, and remain in the taken-for-granted background of your life. An in-law may have very different expectations about what is meant by a gift and what is expected in return. But if you and your partner see eye-to-eye, then together you will be able to withstand the consequences of a gift that changes when it is unpacked.

10. *Who Do You Think You Are?*

The Unexpected Impact of Siblings-in-Law

A DARK image of mother-in-law is stamped on our culture. It is easily recognized and it quickly engages our emotions, like a grotesque character in a fairy tale. The impact of collateral relationships—those between sisters-in-law and brothers-in-law—is more diffuse, hidden, and hard to grasp. But these in-law relationships, too, are potentially powerful bonds, often supportive and liberating, sometimes infuriating and full of conflict. They combine the best and the worst elements of sibling bonds and in-law bonds.

Brothers-in-law and sisters-in-law sit in the shadow of blood siblings—those extraordinary bonds of love and rivalry that have long been recognized as staple features of the human world. This distinctive bond, with its heady mix of competitiveness, protectiveness, antagonism, and affection, lasts well beyond the childhood days of roughhousing and whining over what's fair and what isn't fair. Throughout adulthood, siblings demand from one another acts of loyalty and protectiveness; they take pride in one another's successes; equally, one another's successes trigger rivalry. Siblings connect and compete over just about everything, including partners and children.

A wife may resent her sister-in-law's closeness to her husband. Here, too, the urgent demand to be the "only woman" may give rise to resentments, both small and big. Or a wife might be irritated by her sister-in-law's insider status among her in-laws. Her sister-in-law effortlessly wins approval from a family that sidelines her. A husband may bristle at the deference his wife shows her brother. He may feel undermined by the special value a brother-in-law has in his wife's family. He may resent a brother-in-law's power to exercise her family's authority. Or he may resent the protectiveness and love that his wife offers her brother. The competition for love and status extends from blood siblings to in-laws.

Siblings often influence how we behave to our parents. We may take particular care to phone our mother if we think our brother is likely to neglect her. Our sister may persuade us that failing to attend a family occasion is a sin of omission, or she may assure us that the event is optional. Siblings moderate the roles we take as kin keepers, both in childhood and as adults. In midlife, sisters and brothers-in-law join up in assessing and policing care for elderly parents. "Who needs what?" and "Who should do this?" and "Who does the most?" are questions that shape and monitor siblings' family duties. The spouse, having less investment in your parents, may see you as giving more than is reasonable, while your siblings set high standards for the care of your parents, and may want you to do more than is reasonable.

As with all in-laws, these collateral connections run the gamut of expectation and disappointment: "We will be like sisters" or "We'll be a band of brothers" or "We'll form a sibling clan." Often these hopes are realized, but sometimes expectation splits off from experience, leaving us confused and affronted.

Kelly, Jared, and Gail

One of the first things Jared said to Kelly, after they decided to marry, was, "You and Gail will be like sisters."

Gail is two years older than Jared. She is, Jared explains, a protective and bossy sister; she is also smart and attractive. He sees Gail and Kelly as "two peas in a pod."

Kelly's Story

You can imagine how intrigued I was to meet her. Who was this woman who was, in my lover's eyes, so much like me? It was a little like seeing one of his old girlfriends, except this wasn't someone he was leaving behind. This one would be around for life. But I had the same response I've sometimes had when a guy has gone on and on about some past love. You expect someone wonderful, and you end up meeting her and thinking, "What was that all about?" At the same time, you start drawing in the picture. You know? Matching up what you've heard with what you're seeing.

If I stand back, though, I see what he means. First, we have lots of things in common. Second, Jared doesn't see her oddness, or the edge I see in her, because she's his family. So, I take the line: "I know we should be best friends. We have the same interests. We're so alike, professionally at least, and there are strong—well, broad—similarities physically." But we're just not best friends. It just hasn't happened.

That's what I say to him, but it's closer to the truth to say that I knew at our first meeting that we'd never be best friends. And I bet your boots Gail knew that, too. Maybe she knew it even before we met. Maybe she'd have that edge with anyone her brother loved.

I tried at first. I really did. I tried to push all that niggling irritation aside. I talked to her about her work. Because we're in similar fields, people expect us to talk. People think we should have a lot to talk about. So I tried to develop those professional links. I'd even defer to her opinion, and ask her advice on a case I had, just to be nice. But every time I talked to her I'd end up getting annoyed. At first I didn't know why. I thought, well, sure, some people are just annoying. But then I noticed there were these little digs: "Oh, I deal with cases like that the whole time. You just have to use your judgment. It'll come."

Here I was, being gracious, treating her like a professional equal, and she couldn't resist one-upping me!

This was ten years ago, but it's the same routine today. And that makes things worse, because I know what's coming and get all antsy watching out for it. There's something unwholesome when we get together—maybe like those girls you knew at school who you didn't really like, but hung out with just so you could keep an eye on them.

Gail seems to resent every single success I have, no matter how many she has. My mother-in-law is really proud of me, and I'm not sure Gail likes that! The more aware I become of her competitiveness, the more I think, "This isn't good," and "I don't need this," and "This is weird, and could get nasty." So I just back off. Now that I've stopped making an effort, we have very little contact. Now, we don't really talk, even when we meet. And when we do, it's uncomfortable. Jared's mother is ill, and Gail cracks the whip on both her brothers to make sure they check in on her and visit her and get her what she needs. Gail doesn't do much herself, but she sure makes her brothers work.

Gail's Story

The key to understanding any in-law conundrum is to identify the underlying vulnerability. This can be done only by considering each perspective. What, then, is Gail's story?

In Gail's view, Kelly draws Jared away from their mother:

> Jared isn't taking a fair share of responsibility for our mom. This is all down to Kelly. She wants him all for herself. She tells him he's too close to his mother. Her favorite, stupid line is that he needs to separate. But that doesn't stop her from being on the phone to *her* mother three times a day! That selfish streak of hers is taking him away from our mother, and from me.

Gail reflects on the new obligations she feels towards her mother, and her need to involve her siblings, to ensure their mother feels supported during what may be a terminal illness.

> How can Kelly talk about the need to separate when our mother is in this state. It's so cruel! Kelly thinks that what happens in our family doesn't really matter, and she doesn't want Jared drawn into it.

Gail believes that the resentment between her and Kelly dates back to the time Kelly and Jared were having trouble in their marriage.

> Just after their second child was born, Kelly seemed to change. There was always something about her that I didn't

like, but after their son was born, this showed itself to every-one. Jared was really upset when she "turned." She constantly criticized him, and made these ludicrous demands; then, in Kelly's mind, nothing Jared did was right. There were times when he just needed to get away, and be with someone who wasn't giving him such a hard time. It was nice for me. I have to admit this. It was nice getting my little brother back. It had been a long while since we were that close. He'd drop by, maybe scrounge dinner, and we'd share a bottle of wine, and talk.

We didn't just talk about Kelly. Jared and I talk about everything. But we did talk about Kelly, too. I listened, and I liked listening, but I never told him how much I disliked her. Thank goodness, I had enough sense not to say that, because they stayed together, and my speaking out then would be a real uncomfortable thing between us now. Especially now, they're so tight and cozy. But she treats me like *I* was the one who came between them. I'm the wicked sister-in-law.

Of course, she doesn't say that to my face. And Jared hasn't outright told me that she thinks that. But I know she does. We're polite when we meet. Polite—but she's arch and awful. And even though there's this icy politeness, there are flare-ups over little things, like arrangements for a family dinner. She'll set it up and tell me at the last minute, and then she claims that she thought she had already told me about it. *Yeah, sure.*

Or, I'm in the kitchen, my own kitchen, putting stuff away, and she'll say, "Why are doing that?" or "It's better if you do it this way." When that sort of thing goes on and on, I blow up. But these explosions don't clear the air. They just let the bad feelings out of the box for a minute. They just remind us what we really feel.

Clashing Stories

Sisters-in-law Kelly and Gail interact, and clash, on many levels. There is both a sisterly rivalry and a distinctive in-law rivalry. The sister-like rivalry, without the bonds of sisterly affection, kicks in at first meeting. Kelly is disdainful of her husband's admiration for this woman, and uncomfortable with this high opinion.

There is also more general in-law rivalry: "Who matters more—your spouse or your blood family?" Kelly wants Jared's time and energy and attention for her and their children, primarily. Jared's mother's illness has a claim on the family. This makes it difficult to set boundaries, particularly when his sister outlines his obligations to him. So Kelly blames Gail for demanding too much of Jared. Gail's reaction to Kelly's objection is, "Kelly is selfish."

Siblings retain the power to persuade and upset one another throughout their lives. This makes siblings key players in a marriage, and thus part of the inescapable power of in-laws.

Siblings: Why We're Jealous and Why We Love One Another

The significant role siblings play in our lives has only recently come to light. The bond between parent and child has long been known to shape us. The role of siblings has, for a long time, been seen as secondary. But negotiating love and rivalry with our siblings provides crucial experiences in learning how to live in a world with other people—people who need the same things we do, with whom we play, work, and compete.

Siblings compete for any limited family resources, particularly love, attention, and time. They also identify with one another; they usually love one another; and they often protect one another. Sometimes they protect one another from the terrors of the outside world, sometimes from inner fears, and sometimes from the punishments other family members may inflict. But however ready your sibling is to take a punch from someone who is bullying you on the playground, however reassuring a sibling is about the "monsters" lurking in the corners of a darkened bedroom, however protective a sibling is when your parents are angry, he may be equally happy to punch you himself, or arouse those idiosyncratic fears he knows haunt you, or "tell on you" and "get you into trouble" with your parents.

Sibling bonds contain a mix of feelings. One primary feeling is envy; but this envy is tempered with love and identification and protectiveness. At the root of this primitive envy is the fear that this person who is like me, and who shares my interpersonal world, might replace me. Perhaps he will outshine me with his charms, talents, and achievements, and leave me with no place. Deep within sibling rivalry is the fear: "He will take all I have, and I will be nothing."[1]

Familiar complaints about sisters-in-law and brothers-in-law are: "He thinks he can tell my partner what to do" and "She thinks she's better than me" and "She thinks she has a right to know everything about me." These complaints closely resemble complaints about siblings who are "bossy" or "superior" or "nosey." But the underlying complaint is the fear that a partner's sibling will have more of his love or respect or attention or care than you have. This is the vulnerability that underlies sibling-in-law conflict.

Siblings: Close No Matter What

"How far do you live from your in-laws?" is a question that impacts on connection and conflict with parents-in-law.[2] "I have no trouble with my in-laws. They live thousands of miles away" is a familiar retort. Distance, in some cases, makes these relationships easier. There is less likelihood of informal and uncontrollable intrusion, less risk of a drop-by inspection or an opportunistic request. But distance can also give rise to problems. In emergencies, you have to travel; when visits occur, they are longer, and involve more energy and expense.

But distance seldom protects us from collateral in-laws. Even when siblings do not get along, even when they do not often meet, each is interested in the other, each measures herself or himself in part by reference to a sibling. "He's been able to do that; why haven't I?" or "She's been messed up by our parents, but I've managed to survive" or "He has achieved more than me; I'd better get to work!" Distance does not diminish the impact of siblings: Phone conversations often form the backbone of sibling contact, particularly between sisters. The turmoil of sibling rivalry and love is a fixed part of your spouse's life.

Sibling dynamics are remarkably stubborn. The little sister/big sister patterns can emerge, in pristine form, between siblings in their forties, even when adult experiences have changed beyond recognition the relative strengths and weaknesses of childhood. Still, the big sister tells the little sister what to do. Being drawn into past dynamics is part of the pleasure and comfort of families, but this can also be confusing to someone who is not steeped in the family's emotional history.

Big sister Gail stands as family representative and organizer of family gatherings; during her mother's illness, she becomes the kin keeper. Her brothers accept her moral authority; she tells them how often to call and when to visit. Kelly resents Gail's control, and feels that her own influence with her husband is under threat.

Siblings: Competing Loyalties

Loyalties to a spouse and to a parent have weight and power, and part of the marital contract is a promise to balance these. But a sister-in-law or brother-in-law has less incentive to balance loyalties equally. Their loyalty to a parent is paramount. If they think a sibling is bending towards his or her spouse at the expense of a parent, then they may step in to shift the position.

At the same time, siblings-in-law may be susceptible to the ordinary range of niggling jealousies. A daughter-in-law wants to be embraced as the ideal daughter. A son-in-law wants admiration and respect from his parents-in-law. But a parent-in-law's own children also want love, appreciation, admiration, and respect; and sibling rivalry may be ignited when your own parent finds too much to admire in your sister-in-law. In those competitive undercurrents, where our less good, less civilized doubts and demands may flourish, old pleasures of telling tales on a sibling, or forming an alliance with a parent against a sibling, may prove irresistible.

Some of the most bitter in-law conflict is enacted behind the scenes. The stories we hear about people radically change our views of them. We tell enhancing stories and protective stories and angry stories to make sense of our own emotions. The power to shape your own stories about people in your family is exercised in small daily acts of communication. Trusting what people, particularly people in our family, say is basic to our personal lives. Yet small distortions and omissions can make all the difference between a trustworthy and an untrustworthy report. When descriptions of what happened, and who said what and why, are untested, their power goes unchallenged. Blood relatives share stories on trust about who did what in the family, and an in-law's own version can be easily erased from the record.

Hearing the stories that are told behind our backs can create a distorted world parallel to the one we experience. Harriet feels that, among her in-laws, her version of events is constantly undermined. "My sister-in-law and I exchange some words, and then she runs to tell my mother-in-law that I said this or that, and then when I hear about it from my husband, it's something else." She gets a "sudden punch" of simultaneous recognition and disbelief; she can locate the episode, but is amazed by the distortion of detail.

Grumbles and complaints that remain in shadow carry a special potential for damage. By the time we hear about them, the biased version has wreaked havoc on others' goodwill. The distorted story hardens into others' schemas of "who we are." We fear that an in-law can, with her verbal weapons, change the emotional map that others use to guide their interactions with us.

Family members are particularly good at telling one another stories and shaping one another's memories. Siblings play a special role as witnesses to our past. We combine our efforts to piece together family portraits and family histories. "What happened when?" and "Who said what?" are just a few of the basic blocks of sibling-talk, as sisters and brothers check up on their experiences, and match and challenge one another's memories. Together they construct a family history; siblings share and revise family stories throughout their lives.

Stories bind families together. When an in-law challenges these stories, they are seen as a betrayer. They are insiders who harbor an outsider's view. Their perspective can be unnervingly sharp, and disturb the loyalty that family stories enforce. With a partner, we negotiate different views, with more or less grace. But a sibling-in-law has less ready-made empathy with customary family views. "How dare you see my parents in that way!" and "You don't understand where my brother came from" emerge through the gaps between unmatched stories.

Sibling Rivalry Among Siblings-in-Law

Siblings-in-law sometimes compete just like siblings do for approval from the older generation. Michelle, at the age of sixty-nine, discovered for the first time the forces of sibling rivalry through the endless competitions among her three daughters-in-law:

> I was an only child, so I was the one and only kid in a family with lots of older people—parents, grandparents, and two aunts, but I was the only child. I didn't know what it was to compete for things—at least not in a family, anyway. I had three children—three sons—and even though I saw them fight, I didn't see real envy—not until they married and had children of their own, and now I see it everywhere. My sons are ever watchful of which grandchild I appear to

like best. My middle son has the youngest children, and he thinks I've become jaded. He thinks I'm no longer excited by a new grandchild! He thinks I have a special relationship with his older brother's second child that I'll never have towards him.

He's told me this—not in a nasty or sulky way, just conversational, exploring things, you know. He tells me he's only saying this because his wife keeps saying this. I never thought about it in that way, and had to think, and I knew I had to be careful, but this was—well—it made me uneasy, because it's not obviously *not* true! I do have a special love for my six-year-old granddaughter. There's no two ways about it. She's a darling, and I love her like no other. But it's a private thing, so I didn't say that. And no one would think that from how I act. You know? No one's ever going to see me do anything other than what's fair. Not while I'm alive, and not while I'm dead. There will be no difference in what I leave to her, and to the rest. And that I could tell him, and I did.

But those women—my three daughters-in-law. What's with them? Each of them wants me to think she's the best daughter-in-law to me. They're competing, competing for the love and attention of a mother-in-law! Who would have thought it? And I see they don't get on with each other, and that makes me uneasy. Here, they all come to visit me on the Cape, all at the same time, usually, so there's a lot of noise going on, a lot of background stuff, but I can see their schoolyard games, the little superiorities they lay claim to, the little put-downs. I sometimes think that when I die, the real battle will then rage. Who gets what, and maybe even more important, who was my favorite. Sometimes I'd just like to box their ears. But who knows? Maybe it's not really about me. Maybe they're competing over children, or over husbands. You know: Who got the best son? I can see things going on, but can't catch hold of what it is. Not quite catch it, anyway.

Michelle's daughters-in-law weigh up, in a sibling-like way, the relative dollops of affection she gives to each grandchild; they also measure their own children's merits against those of their nephews and nieces:

Kathe, Jonah's wife, is always so quick to say "Prya was walking by his age" when I'm sitting with Wendy's son. Then she'll go, "Prya, show grandma what you just made," if I have the temerity to be caught up in admiration of Josie's drawings—she's a talented one, she has real talent for drawing. But Kathe will also stoop down to comfort any one of them that's crying or bored, and sort them out. Mind you, there's that oh so satisfied expression on her face when she stands up and looks around to see if people notice that she's sorted it all out, unbidden, but it isn't just show. That's a daughter-in-law and a half, I tell you.

Michelle worries about the impact of their competition on her sons:

It's like they need a parent's focus to keep the lid on that rivalry. Like children who keep a rein on their jealousy because mother's watching. I keep hoping they'll grow out of it—because, really, it's so childish. But then I remember they're not children, and are not likely to grow up more than they are now. It worries me, like I said, how it will be when I'm not around. Maybe things will improve, but I worry what those sisters-in-law might do to the whole family.

The rolling force of in-laws has a long reach.

Siblings and Their In-Laws

Siblings eye up one another over many things, and however much they enjoy one another's company, however proud they are of one another's achievements, they remain competitive. Much conflict among siblings-in-law is shaped by the sibling rivalries that never quite die. Most of us learn to appreciate rather than envy our brothers and sisters. Most of us come to view their achievements and assets as part of our own broader network of achievements ("I have a sister who can do this!"), but we also want as much as our siblings. In-laws themselves can become points of comparison and references in uneasy competition: "Is my brother-in-law better than my husband?" Of course, the self-protective mind promptly searches for a defense strategy. Rita defuses envy with criticism; she is quick to find fault with her successful brother-in-law for "not being nice enough to my sister." John eases his wife's uneasy rivalry with her sister by describing his sister-in-law as "irritating" and "brittle." Our partners may help us manage those lingering rivalries by being skeptical of our siblings' successes and immune to their charms.

But sometimes siblings are jealous about one another's in-laws. The strange connections and disjunctions between sisters and their overlapping families are beautifully mapped in Martha McPhee's autobiographical essay, "Longing for In-Laws." At a Christmas party, Martha recognizes, at once, the man she will love. She challenges her sister to identify "the one," and her sister spots him immediately, makes a beeline for him, and warms him up by flirting with him herself. Mark cannot resist the double approach, and "Thus began the overwhelming gravitational pull of my family, which sucked Mark in immediately and entirely."[3]

Mark's parents have died, and his siblings are scattered, and while Mark gets to know her family, Martha cannot get to know his. Everyone tells Martha that not having in-laws is a reprieve. They remind her how lucky she is not to have in-laws. But Martha does not feel lucky. She feels deprived of a proper knowledge of her partner. We want to know someone we love, and getting to know them also involves getting to know their history, their family, and seeing our loved one in his relatives. We need to know our in-laws to satisfy our eager curiosity about who our partner really is.

Martha's more streamlined family makes her life easier, but also offers her less. "At holidays I am jealous of my sisters," she writes, "who all have somewhere else to go." The places they go and the things they do seem exciting and romantic. She is intrigued by the games her sisters play with their in-laws, and is envious. Her siblings, with their overlapping families, have something she lacks.

We sometimes need sibling rivalry to assess the value of what we have. Martha McPhee reminds us that, whatever problems and irritations they may bring, overlapping families, with their sisters and brothers-in-law, extend our lives.

OVERVIEW

We grow up thinking that we share the same family with our siblings. So, when our sibling marries, we have vested interests in their choice.

- In our protective mode, we wonder, "Is he good enough for my sibling?"
- In our competitive mode, we ask, "Is my sibling now better off than I am?"

Siblings are ever watchful of one's status vis-à-vis that of the other, and the questions "Does this match give her more than me?" and "Does this match threaten my status?" are teased out between siblings and their partners.

- Alongside sibling rivalries is the familiar question we ask as we acquire in-laws: "How will this new family bond change the relationship I have with my sibling?"

Then come follow-on questions: "Will my sibling still be loyal to me and my family?" and "Will I have the love and attention I need from my sibling?" and "Will I still be able to influence my sibling?"

EXERCISES
for Managing Conflict with Our Siblings-in-Law

Conflict with our sibling's partner, and conflict with our partner's sibling, tend to be particularly unpredictable. They wax and wane, and take you by surprise. When they strike, however, the primary question is, as always, "Who is vulnerable, and why?"

This question can be rooted out with a series of reflective questions:

- Who feels threatened by a change in a valued relationship?
- Are you uneasy lest the sibling closeness will edge you out?

- Is your sibling-in-law trying to demonstrate a special, superior bond?
- Do you feel that your sibling-in-law is putting their blood family first, at the expense of yours?
- Do you feel you are losing influence on your partner, and a sibling is taking over?

The answers to these questions may be clarified if you draw a diagram of loyalty pulls between sibling and spouse. The diagram should include you and your partner on one side of the page and all your in-laws on the other side of the page. This will help you explain the complex mix of fears and frustrations to your partner. Once the source of the conflict is identified, it is easier to deal with it. Sometimes simply expressing your concern to a partner will reconfigure the dynamic.

11.   *Are We Still Family?*
Divorce and Connection

IN-LAWS come to us with marriage. Their power slips upon us, and settles in unexpected places in our emotional world. But do in-laws slip away from us if a marriage ends? Does that strange intimacy persist after divorce? And what of those complex affinities and tensions that develop in the course of marriage? How do links with children and grandchildren shape kinship after the legal bond is dissolved?

There is no single pattern of in-laws' responses to former in-laws. Some representative experiences are

"This divorce gives my mother-in-law an excuse to justify her dislike of me."

"I never understood how callous and scheming my in-laws really were at heart until my marriage started to sour."

"The best thing about being divorced is that I don't have to deal with my in-laws anymore. I don't have to think of them as family."

But representative, too, is Jane's remark:

"The hardest thing about getting divorced was losing contact with his family. It deprives me of people I really value."

And for parents-in-law, responses range from

"My only disappointment is that she did not divorce him sooner" to

"The day I heard they had separated was the worst of my life. He was my most difficult son, and she was the best thing that happened to him. I'm sad for him, and I'm sad because I'll simply miss having that wonderful woman as my daughter-in-law."

Divorce is not a single event with the single outcome of a dissolved partnership between two people. It is a process, consisting of several shifting and overlapping stages. The emotional stages that precede a divorce may last three months or thirty years; this is the time during which at least one of the couple identifies the marriage as intolerable. Subsequently, each reacts to the other's emotions. Legal wrangles and financial battles add to the tension, during which family and social alliances are reconfigured. This whirlwind pulls in the children, who see the fabric of their emotional life torn apart; and the parents of each member of the couple are also knocked by this storm. In-laws become ex-in-laws, and both alliances and divisions take new shape.

Linny, Martin, Denise, and Ron: Reversal of the Good-Behavior Syndrome

Linny had been married six years when she decided she would no longer live with a man she described as "constantly critical of me and everything I do, and always undermining me." She had had an affair; her husband, Martin, had had several affairs. But the real break point was "the day-to-day stuff, the sheer annoyance that he broadcasts when I'm around, telling me I'm doing

something wrong, whether it's chopping onions or getting car
insurance or just watching television."

Her parents knew nothing about their daughter's acute dis-
satisfaction with her marriage until its downhill stretch.

My mother had the highest opinion of Martin. He was their
dream son-in-law. A class above them. A good earner. Sorry,
I think my mom would say, "a good provider." He is in good
shape physically. *And* he has good manners. I'm not sure
they didn't think he was too good for me, but they certainly
thought I was lucky to have him. I used to think that was
funny. But it meant I had all this disinformation to fight
through. My mother was telling me things weren't as bad as
I was saying they were. "Of course he loves you." As though
she knows what's going on better than I do! To get through
to her was a real problem.

That's all different, now. Now my dad really hates him. I
mean, really hates him. He says he'd like to poison him. We
got back together for a while, and it was pretty stiff. Poor
Martin. It made me see why from his point of view a dinner
with the in-laws could be hell.

The helplessness parents feel when a child's marriage falls
apart often heightens anger. Even though the anger is protective, their child may have a divided response. "I still love him,"
Linny explains. "I'm very angry at him, but it hurts me when
other people go the silly route—about him being a bastard,
or shaking their heads and muttering, "*men*." I don't want to
become one of those bitter women who hates her ex. And he's
still my son's dad." In Linny's father's view, however, Martin has
hurt their daughter, and nothing else matters.

Revising the Emotional History

In the thick of their own grief, with their feverish empathy for their own child, parents are quick to blame a divorce on an in-law. Money, with its symbolic and practical power, fuels hostility, and Linny's father, Ron, calculates the financial support he has provided for the couple, and pressures Linny to reclaim that in the divorce settlement. "I never meant even one penny of the money I gave them to be his and not hers," he explains.

Ron cannot remember ever having a high opinion of Martin. "I can't remember ever really liking him," Ron says of his former son-in-law. "I just tried to, for Linny's sake."

Memory is carried along by current emotions. With hindsight, a son-in-law or daughter-in-law takes on the features of a stranger and usurper. "There was always something I didn't like about her" and "I never thought he was right for you" are admissions that often come in the wake of divorce. The protective rage and sense of insult shape memories. Former doubts that were mere wisps take on a solidity they might never have actually had before. "I never really took to him" and "There was always something about him that bothered me," Denise says, oblivious now to her former idealization of the perfect son-in-law.

The Standard Story of In-Laws and Divorce

Families live under a shared emotional skin, and an insult to one is felt by others. Parents, too, feel rejected and betrayed when a son or daughter is divorced. Their anger is both empathic and direct.

Parents may be frightened and disappointed, too, by the changing configuration of the family. They also suffer from the breakup. They worry about their own son or daughter, about their grandchildren, and about themselves.

The ensuing responses are familiar, and activate conflict in familiar ways:

- self-justifying criticism ("I am angry with you for rejecting my daughter; therefore you must be bad")
- self-justifying criticism by proxy ("If my son or daughter is treating you badly, then you must deserve it")
- parental bias (excludes empathy for anyone outside the bloodline)

There are, however, surprising variations in responses to in-laws during the process of divorce.

Two Sets of Parents-in-Law; Two Different Reactions

On the day Gerry revealed to Alice that he was deeply in love with one of his clients, they had been married for five years, and had a three-year-old son. As they struggled with the rapid meltdown of their partnership, their priorities were to maintain their own sanity, and their son's well-being. They were buffeted, too, by shifting identities: Gerry felt he was transformed from family man to divorced father and new lover. Alice was transformed from a competent wife and mother to bewildered divorcée who suffered uncontrollable crying spells several times a day. She says she was "in mourning not only for my marriage but also for the person I thought I was." The collateral damage to both sets of parents was unforeseen. "My mother-in-law became a nemesis, with a power over me I cannot fathom," Gerry reflected.

> "No one does this and feels good," he explained. "I knew it was going to be rough with Alice. I knew I was going to feel awful. My parents aren't thrilled to bits, either. But with Alice's folks, I'm a real bastard, and nothing but a bastard.

Gerry mourns the loss of his father-in-law's good opinion:

> "I loved Alice's dad. He's always been so good-humored and friendly. He really took me in, and became a big and a comfortable part of my life. He looks at me now with this puzzled sadness. He's sort of searching for the good person he lost. But Alice's mother looks at me as though I'm the very devil."

As Gerry grapples with his own conscience, he highlights a theme familiar in the mother-in-law jokes told by male comedians of the twentieth century. He sees his mother-in-law as the severe judge. He is uneasy in her presence and blames her for this dark vision of himself.[1]

Sometimes in-law tensions unexpectedly retreat during the process of divorce. Parents-in-law engage in a *compensating strategy* to maintain the bonds of kinship even after divorce. As kin keepers they try to mitigate the split in the family. Alice also experiences a rapidly changing relationship with her mother-in-law, but with a very different outcome.

> From the beginning, I knew that Becky, my mother-in-law, saw me as a temporary add-on. At first I tried to be friends with her. I tried to make myself interesting. But her eyes would glaze over if I talked for longer than a nanosecond.

Here was this woman who was open and active in so many ways—just not with me.

Now, it's a totally different story. She's sick about what's happened between me and Gerry, and she seems to blame him more than me. She's become my protector, which is an amazing reversal. She checks up on me every few days, takes Guy to the playground, takes him swimming. She even took us shopping the other day. She's never before made such an effort with me.

Tracing vulnerability to its source is key to understanding in-law relationships, and this rule also applies to in-law relationships as they are reconfigured by divorce. Becky now focuses on protecting her grandson and maintaining contact with him: "That sweet little boy is all I can think about. I'll keep an eye on him and make sure I tell him over and over again, in all the ways I can, that he's part of this family. And that means his mom is, too."

Support from grandparents can go a long way towards softening the harsh effects of divorce on children,[2] but Becky's compensating strategy may also stem from a more self-interested calculation. As paternal grandparents, Alice's parents-in-law are at significant risk of losing contact with their grandchild.[3] Maternal grandparents have easier access to their grandchildren, because it is the mother who tends to be the gatekeeper, deciding who her children can or cannot see. About 40 percent of grandparents want more contact with their grandchildren than they in fact have.[4] A good relationship with Alice will ensure she retains contact with her grandson. As always, understanding in-law relationships, in any of their many guises, depends on understanding the passionate love bonds between blood relations.

Do In-Laws Cause Divorce?

The primary reason why understanding the dynamics of in-law relationships is crucial to our well-being is that we can expect our in-laws to play a significant role in our lives. Common assumptions about the decline of the family are countered by the tenacity of the extended family. The care of one generation for another is robust and long-lasting.

But does the power of the vertical family—parents and children and grandchildren—have a weakening effect on the horizontal family? Do in-laws cause divorce?

A Tale from Italy

A divorce lawyer working in Italy was alarmed by the number of marriages that seemed to founder on in-law relationships. Couples who came to her as their marriage disintegrated often complained of an intrusive or overbearing mother-in-law.[5] When the divorce rate in Italy increased by 45 percent from 2000 to 2002, policy-makers were so concerned that they set to work investigating the causes of divorce. They found that among the triggers of divorce were immaturity, money, and infidelity; but 30 percent of divorces in Italy apparently failed because of in-law tensions.[6] The primary tension between in-laws was between the son's mother and his wife.

This tension, between two women, triggers divorce only if a wife feels that she has no power in her own home, that her private space is unprotected, and that her needs have no impact in daily family life. In-law despair can destroy a marriage only through the marriage itself.

Even apparently cut-and-dried cases of "mother-in-law inva-sion" come down to a triangular relationship. Luisa catches sight of this as she tries to maintain her equilibrium while accommo-dating her newly widowed mother-in-law in her home. Eventu-ally, she concludes:

> I'll have to leave if I'm going to survive. In one way, this is mad, because I still love my husband, but he seems to have abandoned me. What I feel isn't real to him. He thinks I'm strong and his mother is weak, and so I should accept what she needs. When I try to tell him how bad this situation is for me, he gets angry and goes out. So I don't know whether he has destroyed my marriage, or my mother-in-law has.

The greatest risk to a marriage through in-law conflict stems from a failure to combine different loyalties. "Whose side are you on?" signals abandonment. "Why are you protecting your mother or father, and not me?" springs from being marginalized when you expect to be the significant other in your partner's life. Your partner responds with equal outrage: "Why are you asking me to choose?" and "Why won't you help me do my duty towards my parents?" To reduce the risk of damage from divided loyalties, we need to understand the role that in-laws are playing in our marriage, and find ways of working with our partner to maintain these connections while protecting our well-being. Without these skills, our marriage may be at risk.

Regret at Losing In-Laws

There is no single story for any in-law relationship, and no single pattern of in-law experiences. Living with in-laws is sometimes wonderful, and sometimes awful. Leaving them can trigger relief, or lingering regret. Looking back on a marriage that he "stumbled into in the stupid haze of youth," Steve describes an acute sense of loss; divorce severed the bond with his former father-in-law. Their shared sense of humor, their easy companionship, and the touching acceptance his father-in-law offered him were lost as his marriage disintegrated. "It's strange," Steve reflects, "how quickly you get into another family; it has a ready-made structure, and it closes in on you, nicely, just because you've married their daughter. And when you're not married to her anymore, the feelings are still there but without the relationship."

In the right conditions, family feelings take hold very quickly. As Steve notes, the psychological structure is in place. Kin has an impact, immediate and profound. Most couples think about themselves and their children when they consider divorce; the powerful effects on the overlapping family take you by surprise.

OVERVIEW

Divorce is not a single event but a long and difficult process that impacts in-law bonds and feelings. Expected patterns of change include

- confirmed hostility ("I knew he was no good")
- revised, negative history ("I never really liked her")
- disillusionment ("I never thought she could behave like this")
- anger ("How dare she treat my child like this")

There are also unexpected in-law responses to divorce, which include

- protectiveness ("I feel sorry for her, and don't want her to be lonely")
- strategic closeness ("If she shuts me out of her life, I'll lose contact with my grandchildren")
- regret ("I loved my in-laws" and "I've lost a valuable bond in losing them")
- anger, with a twist ("My son doesn't realize how good she was for him. I can't believe he treated her like this")

EXERCISES
for Managing In-Law Conflicts
During the Process of Divorce

Divorce unleashes anger in everyone it touches—the couple, the couple's children, and the couple's two sets of parents. Under anger's spell, we often long for some kind of revenge. There is no point to this battle. The rough guide to the power of in-laws suggests you take the long view, reduce expectations, and wait to see the fallout. The most important thing to remember is that grandparents play an important and positive role in children's lives, and it is the mother who often acts as gatekeeper to the grandparents.

Here are some reasonable aims:

- "I want to offer positive support to my daughter or son."
- "I want to maintain a relationship with my in-law that will make sense if the marriage does not dissolve."
- "I want to keep the doors open to see my grandchildren."

You may be very angry and hurt; and, in the grip of these feelings, projection and the self-justifying principle can gain control. When we are angry and hurt, we blame another person, and emphasize that person's faults. According to the self-justifying principle, disapproval becomes more entrenched the more hostile we become. So, ask yourself,

"What will I gain by sticking with my anger?"

and

"What will I lose?"

While engaging in these exercises, be pragmatic and identify your aims. Ask yourself,

"Do I want to protect my own child?"

If so, follow-on questions include:

"Will hating my former son-in-law or daughter-in-law help?"

and

"What family connections do I want to maintain?"

and

"Can I play a useful role as lynchpin to all family members?"

Think about protectiveness:

"How can I cushion the blows of divorce to people who matter to me?"

and

"Might everyone I care about be better off if I maintain a family-like connection with a former son- or daughter-in-law?"

Parents and parents-in-law may feel helpless in the storm of divorce. But the breakdown of a couple's relationship is only one thread in the family network. In-laws, including former in-laws, can help to keep a family strong.

12.

Getting Along and Looking Forward

Rifts and Reparation Across the Life Span

THE POWER of in-laws changes over the course of a marriage. We have seen how Rosa, so territorial about her husband during the first years of marriage and determined to show her mother-in-law that she was the primary woman in James's life, relaxes when she has her own children. The early competition eventually becomes "bizarre and unnecessary." She comes to enjoy her mother-in-law's company, and hopes to make amends for those early years of power play.

There is Ian, who bristled at his in-laws' constant cold assessments of every career move, and could "see" the chiseled features of their disapproval even when he spoke to them on the telephone. Subsequently, he came to value their determination and their high standards, and to realize what an important part they played in raising his own aspirations.

There is Grace, who was initially irritated by her mother-in-law's reserve, and complained to her husband about low-key animosity, until she realized that her own mood swings and enthusiasms might be tiring for those close to her, and that her children would benefit from being close to relatives with a different, more even temperament.

There are parents-in-law who initially believe that a son or daughter "could have done better," and are disappointed in their choice, but realize, many years on, that the chosen partner has qualities that "lasted." For many people, in-laws become a combination of friend and relative.

Over time, people often learn to appreciate and respect their in-laws, to get the most out of them, and to avoid those interactions that generate a negative charge. Yet sometimes in-law relationships become "impossible." Each interaction leads to humiliation and frustration. The only solution may be to insist on an in-law version of divorce.

Reasons for Divorcing In-Laws

Among the forty-nine families in my studies, six couples seriously considered cutting off all contact with at least one of their in-laws. These extreme cases arose when a couple was unable to manage disruptive, manipulative, or cruel behavior.

Bea, Mike, and Valerie: Escalating Intrusiveness

Intrusive in-laws may be the stuff of jokes, but there is nothing funny about being unable to control boundaries in one's own home. Bea describes how her "thoughts bang away in [her] head" when she thinks up strategies for managing her mother-in-law:

> She calls constantly, and she demands that we come to visit her. However many times we do this, she is not satisfied. When we are there, we have to do everything her way, and

if we don't—well, she makes life miserable. Sometimes she shouts and sometimes she cries, but either way, it's awful. Even if we give in, and we always do, we have to spend hours placating her. Sometimes we think she's calmed down; then suddenly it will start all over again. It's so exhausting. I think it would be better if I just gave up seeing her, and let my husband go himself.

The misery spreads beyond the time they spend together, because Bea keeps trying to think of a new approach:

I keep thinking of things she's likely to ask us to do. Then I get my answer ready. But each time I think it through, I know she'll fly back with some wily countermove. Anything I say, she'll squash it. There's no argument I can win with her. Because if she doesn't get her way, she'll sulk around Mike. And even though he sort of understands what's going on, he gives in to her."

The anxiety leading up to visits with her mother-in-law is all absorbing. It involves what is called "left-hemisphere brain chatter," or loops of thinking and planning that destroy our equilibrium as we visualize over and over again possible scenarios, thinking of ways to gain control in a situation we know will be stressful.

Like many people, Bea dislikes the person she becomes in the midst of in-law conflict. "I'm usually a reasonable and tolerant person. I don't usually hold a grudge. But with my mother-in-law I get carried away by rage, and I waste so much mental energy searching for some way to get a grip on the situation. But I know I never will. I can't stand how mad I get with Mike, and I can't stand how edgy I get before I see my mother-in-law.

I know all this just sets me up to get annoyed with her. So, it's better if I just step out of the picture and let Mike deal with her by himself. She must give him hell when he visits without me. But he doesn't talk about it."

For five years, Bea has not visited Valerie. When Valerie visits Mike, Bea makes sure there is a written agreement with Mike as to when he will make the four-hour drive back to return his mother to her home (extensions to the visit are not allowed); and he has not broken that agreement. Here the mother/son bond continues, but daughter-in-law and mother-in-law are at an impasse.

Roz, Patrick, and Fiona: Necessary Distance

In-law conflict can also arise from protectiveness towards a partner. When your in-laws are systematically cruel to their own son or daughter, the spouse feels anger and outrage.

Soon after Roz and Patrick married, Patrick took a realtor's exam, and they then went on vacation. On the third morning of their vacation, they walked out of their cabin to find something stuck to the car windshield.

> At first I thought it was a parking ticket, which was odd, because we were in the middle of nowhere. When I saw what it was, I would have been glad to trade it for a thousand dollar parking fine! You know what it was? It was a letter from Patrick's mother telling him that they'd got the letter about his exam. They'd decided to open it, and they learned that he'd failed, so put the letter with his grades and the notice that he'd failed right on the windshield. I couldn't believe it! But Patrick got the picture right away. He didn't even see how

weird it was, the way I did, because he sees such humiliating treatment as normal. That made my heart bleed for him.

The realization that Patrick's parents would intrude on his privacy by opening a private letter, and then would disturb his vacation and humiliate him struck Roz as "beyond belief." As these choreographed cruelties persisted, Roz and Patrick together decided they would reduce contact with his parents to a minimum.

Amy Bloom writes about her in-laws' "minginess, their poor-mouthing, their harsh unhappiness." Her hatred can "roil" because it is protective. She herself smarts from the terrible things her in-laws have said to her spouse, and the way their bigotry has hurt her partner: "When they found out she was gay, her mother turned all of her photographs facedown."[1] Amy acts as a buffer to "the fireball of misery" her parents-in-law cause in her partner. That is sometimes the role we play in families: We protect someone we love by standing between them and the people who do not love him enough.

Reconnecting with Love

Anger and pain can cause misery, but they do not necessarily dismantle the enduring structure of the family. After fourteen years of marriage, when they had put the hope of children to one side, Roz discovered she was pregnant. She reflected:

This has made me go back, and rethink everything. I worry how Fiona can be . . . how she can be so nasty, and so good at not seeing how she's hurting someone. But I can't be so cruel as to deprive anyone of their grandchild. And life is too fragile to deny my child contact with a grandmother. I know she loves her son, and I know she'll love her grandchild. I'll just have to watch things, and make sure she doesn't hurt my child, the way she did her own.

Roz and Patrick shift gears again when Patrick's father dies and, soon after, his mother has a mild stroke. Roz explains:

It's amazing how your feelings for someone can change like that. Suddenly Fiona was simply a woman who was ill. She is my husband's mother, and she needed our help. You think anger is real, and then it just gets pushed to the side. She just wasn't the demon I thought she was.

We go to see her pretty much every week. And even when we're not there, there's a lot of organizing from a distance. Sometimes I think it's an emergency, like last week it sounded like the heating packed in, and I made the trip, but the thermostat just needed to be set right. But I keep doing this, and I'll keep doing it as long as she's around.

Ties That Bind

The most entrenched and bitter in-law clashes should not blind us to the range of loving and supportive in-law relationships. "My daughter-in-law is a light in my life. She is strong and brings me such pleasure," says Shirley. And her daughter-in-law, Sally, says, "Shirley gives me more support than my mom. She loves my children as much as I do. She has offered me nothing but pleasure."

Kinship networks support us in the rough and tumble of life. While many of us cannot claim with Sally that our in-laws give us "nothing but pleasure," we need to manage their power, so that we can sustain these networks for the sake of all those we care about.

I began this book by saying that the persistence of the extended family is one of the best-kept secrets of modern times. Extended families constantly exchange mutual aid, especially among women.[2] Complaints and tensions are common, but so are mutual support and care. In her fourth decade of marriage, Mona[3] explains,

> It is important for me to help my husband look after his mother. I couldn't bear it if we didn't offer her what we can. I'm sure if you talked to me twenty years ago you would have heard a very different story. She has aggravated me, and I have felt insulted by a hundred little things she does. But she's one of us—I think my children have taught me that, and I would not want my husband to be burdened by guilt now that she is so needy and frail.

Kinship networks are here to stay. Changing life spans do not merely extend the life of an individual; they extend relationships of care between people. Midlife adults are sometimes called the sandwich generation, the generation in the middle pressed by obligations to a younger and an older generation. Though most elderly people want to remain independent, the medical marvels that prolong life and address specific clusters of physical problems do not ensure independence. This longer period of elderly dependence brings new responsibilities to adult sons and daughters, and to their spouses.

Middle-aged daughters and sons are offering practical, emotional, and financial care to their parents, and to their parents-in-law.[4] The common beliefs that the extended family is in decline, and that elderly people are neglected by their families, are challenged by daily acts of care. Families have always looked after elderly parents; and now that old age is lasting longer than ever, their daughters and sons—some in midlife and some nearly elderly themselves—feel the burden of responsibility and the claims of love. This involves time and money and energy from all the family, but the actual care is usually provided by the women in the family—the daughter and daughter-in-law.

Among the forty-nine families collaborating in my studies, fifteen couples were caring for either a parent or parent-in-law, and in two cases they were caring for a grandparent-in-law following the death of the parents. Some were involved in long-distance care that combined intense organization and occasional hands-on help. Some were involved in daily domestic routines of care, with an elderly parent-in-law sharing their home.

It is estimated that in the United States 15 million adults are caring for their aging parents. In Britain, by the time a woman reaches the age of fifty-nine, she has a fifty-fifty chance of having care responsibilities for an elderly relative.[5]

When adult children care for elderly parents, they reflect on duties that arise from love and attachment. They often welcome the opportunity to reciprocate for past care. Many explain that they would find it unimaginable to get on with their own lives while knowing that a parent is lonely, in pain, or simply in need of daily comfort.

In empathy with a partner, care is often extended to in-laws.

Elder Care: His and Hers

Women remain the lynchpin of family contact, the kin keepers, who carry a "worry burden" of concern about the younger and older generations' health, well-being, and comfort. In spite of the multilayered conflict between mother-in-law and daughter-in-law, daughters-in-law often take charge of routine acts of contact, and drive forward the intricate practicalities of a caring agenda for an elderly in-law. Alison, like many wives, ensured that her husband, Jeff, kept in touch with his mother: "It's her birthday next week. I've got a card. Can you sign it? And maybe flowers this time?" She is the one who reminds him to call his mother, and when to visit her. Alison explains:

> He feels bad if he's not a good son. But he doesn't keep these things in his mind. He'd forget his mother's birthday, and then—well, once upon a time, she would remind him, pretend not to, of course, pretend she was just mentioning it—and then he'd remember he forgot, and feel bad. So I protect him from that. He's a good guy, and there's no reason for him to feel guilty.

The role as kin keeper is not based solely on personal affection. Alison explains that,

> Elsie never really liked me. When I try to be friendly, I can feel this alarm, like I've done something off—like I smell! I'm too big for her. All the women in her family have a different bone structure, and compared to them, I'm a giant. But it's more than that. There's some real genetic difference. Different gene pool, different tribe. I'm too outspoken—or maybe it's just that I speak on my terms and not hers. Anyway, she

and I have never been a good match. So I stay out of things, but I make sure Jeff does what he has to do not to feel bad about himself. He wants to be a good son.

Alison takes the lead in her mother-in-law's care, but Elsie fails to notice. Instead, Elsie's gratitude is directed towards her son alone.

Denial is a form of ingratitude, but it is sometimes understandable. Elderly people often say, "I want to be independent" and "I don't want to be a burden to anyone." Sometimes, by saying this, they stave off their own knowledge of how much others are working on their behalf. They focus on how much they still manage to do for themselves, and ignore the constant worry, and the constant checking up, and the constant support of close relatives. A person who is losing her independence may well work to disguise this from herself, for even frail minds maintain their protective vanity. It can be terrifying for someone with increasing vulnerability to step back to see the entire picture, and say, "This is what I'm asking."

When Elsie was diagnosed with Alzheimer's disease, Alison stepped in to provide support and organize care. Her response to a relative in need, however, is different from a response to a blood relative:

Caring for my own mother would be a totally different thing, because I really love her. And I'd feel better about a lot of stuff if I could say I really loved Elsie, but I don't. I just don't. But you can't let someone in your family neglect themselves. And if I don't arrange her care, no one will. It just won't be done. It's not that Jeff doesn't care. He loves her, and he cares more than I do. But he doesn't focus on the details. He doesn't see

just what she needs, and how to go about fixing things up.
If I didn't do it, Elsie would have to make do, somehow, and
Jeff would feel bad. Besides, how can I neglect my children's
grandmother?

No mother-in-law says to her daughter-in-law, "I want you
to look after me when I am unable to look after myself," yet this
is a role that many daughters-in-law take on. This may be one
layer in the intensity of feeling, a foreshadowing of how power
and vulnerability shifts in families.

Over and over again, we can see how the power of in-laws
resides in the connections our in-laws have to those we love.
Daughters-in-law, like Alison, step up to meet the crises of elder
care because empathy with her husband triggers care for his
mother. The triangle of care—an elderly person in need, a son
who feels responsible for an ailing parent but is overwhelmed
by anxiety, and a wife who wants to support her partner and
who therefore cares for her mother-in-law—completes the life
cycle of in-law intimacy.

A Mother-in-Law in Need

It is unlikely that, on some level, a mother-in-law is not aware
of her potential reliance on her daughter-in-law. The role each
woman is expected to play in the family, the likelihood that a
woman will live longer than her partner and is therefore more
likely to be dependent on her daughter-in-law's care, must register. The power plays that engage many women as they take on
in-law roles may signal an underlying fear of being supplanted,
and a dread of what may lie ahead. While being kin keeper is a
burden and a constraint, it is also a powerful role.

The reluctance to admit the inevitability of dependence is spreading beyond our individualistic Western culture and into cultures, like those of India and China, where caring for elderly relatives was once routine. A current highly popular and influential television series showing in India challenges the previously unquestioned supremacy of the mother-in-law over the daughter-in-law. At the same time, many episodes in the series highlight the complexity and fragility of this relationship, and suggest that, if this relationship shatters, the entire family is threatened with collapse.[6]

In Taiwan, the once traditional structure that underpinned a mother-in-law's power is also shifting. Mrs. Shen, sixty-five years old and living in rural Taiwan, said, "When we were married we cried because we belonged to another family. We had to cook and to serve others. We used to worry: Would they like our cooking? Now [daughters-in-law] are useless. Women today are afraid of their daughters-in-law. They dare not criticize them. If you criticize a daughter-in-law she will run away. Daughters-in-law look at you with ugly faces."[7]

Yet the strange revelation of my studies is that women's care for mothers-in-law exceeds all expectations. The activity of care itself often generates love. "I look at this sweet old woman, and wonder why I was once so hard on her," Roz reflects. "She's so pliant, now. I actually hugged her the other day when she criticized me, because I was glad to get a glimpse of those rough edges I thought were lost. Her illness puts everything on a different level. Love isn't just feeling love. It's knowing you are part of a family. And that's what I'm doing now. I'm just being part of a family."

To grasp the true nature of our lives among in-laws, we have to smash the stereotype of the manipulative, disdainful mother-in-law; but the dark complexity of in-law relationships cannot be denied. Each in-law confronts the other with fears about the balance of loyalty, of power, and of love. What happens when one of that uneasy pair becomes helpless? What is the experience of a mother-in-law who has to turn to her daughter-in-law for support?

In-laws are an inevitable consequence of marriage and of enduring family bonds. The relationships formed, like all family connections, are vastly varied, sometimes supportive and affectionate, sometimes cold, infuriating and destructive. These connections change over the life course and are seldom all that we think they are at any one moment. Family passions have changing, hidden shapes, and constantly take us by surprise. We think we want to be rid of someone, and then discover that we are bereft by their absence. Alison's mother-in-law died during the period of the interviews. In the wake of the "body blow of grief" that followed her mother-in-law's death, Alison realized,

> All the time I was thinking of her as a set of chores I had to do for Jeff, but when Elsie died, I suddenly realized how much my own son was losing in losing her, and I saw Jeff's bewildered grief, and I suddenly fell apart. All the sweet things she said to me and did for me came into focus. It wasn't easy with us. She and I—well, we were never a natural match. But she came to look at me with a kind of curiosity or interest that was a sort of pride, and I liked that. I liked that a lot. It made me feel strong. Our relationship was made up of little things, but it amounted to so much more, because we were family.

The "so much more" that resides within in-law relationships emerges day to day, in endless variety, in each family. If we recognize common patterns of connection and conflict, and gain skills for navigating our own and others' biases, and mutually exercise regard and appreciation for our in-laws, then our family as a whole will be strengthened, and the complex alliances within the family can thrive.

Notes

Introduction

1. "Blood" family is an abbreviated way of referring to parents, children, siblings, grandparents. These relations usually are linked genetically, and reference to "blood" relationships is a colloquial way of indicating primary family relationships. These of course include those who become children and parents and grandparents by adoption or reproductive technology. The psychology underlying the kinship structure in such cases is unlikely to be different.

2. Forty-nine couples and their in-laws: this breaks down to 49 wives and 40 husbands, 49 mothers-in-law, 18 fathers-in-law, and 10 siblings-in-law. Twelve couples were from a study conducted in 1985; 12 couples were from a study conducted in 1999; and 25 couples were from a study conducted between 2005 and 2008.

3. For one strong defense of this method of qualitative research, see Forshaw, "Free qualitative research."

4. See Irwin, "Mother-in-law can't help spoiling"; Frean, "No joke for mother-in-law."

Chapter One

1. Young and Lemos, "Family and kinship revisited."

2. Norton and Miller, *Marriage, Divorce, and Remarriage in the 1990's.*

3. Since 2004, there has been a decline in divorce rates, which may signal a trend.

4. Young and Lemos, "Family and kinship revisited."

5. Baruch and Barnett, "Adult daughters' relationships with their mothers"; Hagestad, "Parent-child relations in later life"; Brooks-Gunn and Fursten-berg, "Long-term implications of fertility-related behavior."

6. Gross, "Elder-care costs deplete savings of a generation."

7. Apter, *The Myth of Maturity*, pp. 19–21.

8. Not every primary family offers mutuality, either; its absence can have a severe impact on emotional health.

9. EU.R.E.S., "Un divorzio ogni quattro minuti."

10. In the United Kingdom, in 2005 there were just under 284,000 marriages (Office for National Statistics, *Social Trends*, p. 20). In the year 2001, there were more than 11.6 million married couple families (Office for National Statistics, *Social Trends*, p. 20). In the United States, in the year 2006 the total number of married couples was 119 million (where the spouse was present) compared to 118.7 million in 2005 (U.S. Census Bureau, 2006; U.S. Census Bureau, 2005).

   In the United States, in 2006 there were 22.8 million divorced couples and 5 million separated couples (U.S. Census Bureau, 2006).

11. Duvall, *In-Laws, Pro and Con*; Horsley, *The In-Law Survival Manual*.

12. Cocola, *Six in the Bed*.

Chapter Two

1. Chabon, "My father-in-law, briefly."

2. Anderson and Middleton, "What is this thing called love?"

3. The currency of this assumption emerges in high-profile discussions of marriage and mothers-in-law. Recently, Cecilia Sarkozy has elicited sympathy for having to deal with an ex-mother-in-law who "never let go of her little boy." See di Giovanni, "Mothers-in-law who are no joke."

4. Waldman, "Dividing a man from his mother," p. 37.

5. Viorst, *Necessary Losses*.

6. Duvall, *In-Laws, Pro and Con*; Horsley, *In-Laws*.

7. Apter, *You Don't Really Know Me*.

8. Phillips, "On becoming a mother-in-law."

9. Waldman, "Dividing a man from his mother," pp. 31–32.

Chapter Three

1. The Ashanti of Ghana. For example, see Fortes, *Marriage in Tribal Societies*.

2. Fortes, *Rules and the Emergence of Society*.

3. Goody, *The Development of the Family and Marriage in Europe*.

4. Wedekind et al., "MHC-dependent mate preferences in humans."

5. Skynner and Cleese, *Families and How to Survive Them*.

6. Pinker, *How the Mind Works*.

7. Fine, *A Mind of Its Own*.

8. The prohibition on face-to-face contact between son-in-law and mother-in-law has been interpreted by anthropologists as an expression of shame: How can you look at the man who is having intercourse with your daughter? The intimacy by proxy that arises between a parent and her son's or daughter's lover is sometimes filled with warmth and sometimes filled with revulsion. Social rules for distancing in-laws might control these powerful feelings (Fortes, *Marriage in Tribal Societies*).

9. Kirkpatrick, *The Family as Process and Institution*.

10. Fine, *A Mind of Its Own*, p. 162.

Chapter Four

1. Apter, "Mother-in-law and daughter-in-law"; Duvall, *In-Laws, Pro and Con*; Horsley, *The In-Law Survival Manual*.

2. This survey was conducted by S. C. Johnson in August 2004. The one thousand participants were selected from the Women's Institute. See Taggart, "Will your bathroom pass the test?"

3. Jack, *Silencing the Self*.

4. Hochschild with Machung, *The Second Shift*.

5. The first study was done in 1985. The second study was completed in 1999. The third study ran from 2005 to 2008.

6. Sweet and Bumpass, National Survey of Families and Households. The average wife does 31 hours of housework a week, while the average husband does 14. When both husband and wife have full-time employment, the wife does 28 hours of housework a week, and the husband 16 hours. In families where the wife stays at home and the husband is in paid employment, the wife spends 15 hours a week caring for their children, and the husband spends 2 hours. In families where both parents are in paid employment, the wife spends 11 hours caring for their children, and the husband spends 3 hours.

7. Baron-Cohen, *The Essential Difference*.

8. Apter and Josselson, *Best Friends*.

9. Ibid.

Chapter Five

1. Either partner can be a habitual stonewaller; either partner can have particular trouble engaging with negative feelings, but since it is more often a man who stonewalls and has trouble renegotiating a relationship with his mother,

the examples I give are based on the more common triangle: son/husband/wife/mother-in-law.

2. Gottman with Silver, *Why Marriages Succeed or Fail.*

3. Apter, *Altered Loves.* See also Youniss and Smollar, *Adolescent Relations with Mothers, Fathers and Friends.*

4. Apter, *You Don't Really Know Me;* Patterson and Forgatch, *Parents and Adolescents Living Together.*

Chapter Six

1. Gates, "Hating Hillary."

2. Walton and Cohen, "Stereotype lift."

3. Phillips, "On becoming a mother-in-law."

4. Ibid.

5. For an account of how self-consciousness and deliberate effort interfere with our judgement, see Gladwell, *Blink,* and Fine, *A Mind of Its Own.*

6. Tannen, *You Just Don't Understand.*

7. Bateson, *Steps to an Ecology of Mind.*

8. Eaker et al., "Marital status, marital strain." In Eaker's study, 4,000 women and men were asked whether they expressed their feelings directly or contained their thoughts and feelings during a marital quarrel; 32 percent of the men said they used self-silencing as a strategy, as did 235 of the women in the study. The participants' health was monitored for a ten-year period. Women who said they did not speak out during quarrels were four times as likely to die during the ten-year study period as were the women who described themselves as outspoken. The difference in quarrelling strategies (outspoken or self-silencing) had no effect on the health of the men in the study.

9. Baron et al., "Hostility, anger, and marital adjustment." See also Parker-Pope, "Marital spats, taken to heart."

10. Duras, "The stolen pigeons."v

11. Seligson, *A Little Bit Married.*

Chapter Seven

1. Fine, *A Mind of Its Own.*

2. This family was introduced in Chapter Five of this book.

3. Shapiro, "My mother's four rules," p. 171.

4. Fine, *A Mind of Its Own,* p. 14.

5. This family was first introduced in Chapter Two of this book.

6. Ibid.

7. Burger and Huntzinger, "Temporal effects on attribution."

8. See Chapter Four.

9. Bloom, "Dead, thank God," p. 62.

10. Shapiro, "My mother's four rules," p. 171.

11. This family was first introduced in Chapter Four of this book.

12. Fine, *A Mind of Its Own*, p. 28.

13. Dweck, *Mindset*.

Chapter Eight

1. In both the United States and the United Kingdom, children report greater closeness to their mothers' parents than to their fathers' parents. Paternal grandparents sometimes have difficulty maintaining contact with their grandchildren when the couple divorce. Conflict with a daughter-in-law can also reduce paternal grandparents' access to their grandchildren. For example, see Dunn, *Family Relationships*.

2. Fischer, "Mothers and mothers-in-law."

3. Hawkes, "The grandmother effect."

4. Of the grandparents, 148 were grandmothers and 33 were grandfathers. Young and Lemos, "Family and kinship revisited."

5. Grandparents Association, www.grandparents-association.org.uk.

Chapter Nine

1. Goody, *Kinship*, p. 120.

2. Hitchcock, "Rising number of dowry deaths in India."

3. The first instances of bride burning occurred in the latter part of the twentieth century. They are not part of the ancient dowry tradition.

4. Horsley, *The In-Law Survival Manual*.

5. Apter, *The Myth of Maturity*.

6. Horsley, *The In-Law Survival Manual*, p. 198.

Chapter Ten

1. Apter, *The Sister Knot*.

2. Instituto Nazionale di Statistica, "Matrimoni, separazioni e divorzi."

3. McPhee, "Longing for in-laws," p. 44.

Chapter Eleven

1. In an autobiographical piece "I married my mother-in-law," Peter Richmond turns this around. His initial cocky optimism that his "Ivy-league

pedigree would outweigh what I generously referred to as my personal eccentricities, such as generally giving less than a damn about anyone else" (Richmond, "I married my mother-in-law"), soon gives way to an awareness of his mother-in-law's shrewd scepticism. Peter Richmond projects his own ethical standard onto his mother-in-law; she ends up as guardian of his conscience; she steadies him, and he knows that if he marries into her family, it will have to be for life. Peter Richmond wanted to live up to this high moral standard. Gerry cannot meet it, and so dreads all contact with his mother-in-law. She brings him face-to-face with aspects of himself he would prefer to ignore.

2. Dunn, *Family Relationships*.

3. Ibid.

4. Grandparents Plus, www.grandparentsplus.org.uk.

5. Paola Mescoli Davoli, a lawyer practicing in Italy, was so concerned by the number of couples seeking divorce, and by the frequency of complaints that a husband's mother was instrumental in the deterioration of the marriage, that she set up now-thriving workshops on how to behave as a mother-in-law, particularly how to avoid interfering in the couple's home life, and how to desist from making comments that undermine a daughter-in-law's position as wife.

6. Institute EU.R.E.S., November 2006.

Chapter Twelve

1. Bloom, "Dead, thank God," p. 60.

2. Young and Lemos, "Family and kinship revisited."

3. This family was first introduced in Chapter Six of this book.

4. The value of women's care of elderly relatives in the United Kingdom alone is 57.4 billion pounds: CarersUK, *Without us . . . ?*

5. George, "It could be you."

6. There is also some evidence that such programs improve women's autonomy, since they engage in a range of issues that validate women's experience. See Jensen and Oster, *The Power of TV*.

7. Gallin, "The intersection of class and age."

Bibliography

Alvarez, H. P. "Grandmother hypothesis and primate life histories." *American Journal of Physical Anthropology* 113, no. 3 (November 2000): 435–50. Published Medical Index (PMID) 11042542.

Anderson, Alun, and Lucy Middleton. "What is this thing called love?" *New Scientist* (April 29, 2006): 32–34.

Apter, Terri. *Altered Loves: Mothers and Daughters During Adolescence.* New York: Ballantine, 1991.

———. "Elder care and midlife women." Paper presented at "Equality at the turning point: Reconciling family life and working experience," conference hosted by the European Commission and ASDO, Rome, June 3, 2004.

———. "Mother-in-law and daughter-in-law: friendship at an impasse." Paper presented at British Psychological Society London Conference, December 20, 1999.

———. *The Myth of Maturity: What Teenagers Need from Parents to Become Adults.* New York: W. W. Norton, 2001.

———. *The Sister Knot: Why We're Jealous, Why We Fight, and Why We Love Each Other No Matter What.* New York: W. W. Norton, 2007.

———. *You Don't Really Know Me: Why Mothers and Daughters Fight, and How Both Can Win.* New York: W. W. Norton, 2004.

Apter, Terri, and Ruthellen Josselson. *Best Friends: The Pleasures and Perils of Girls' and Women's Friendships.* New York: Crown, 1998.

Baron, K. G., T. W. Smith, J. Butner, J. Nealey-Moore, M. W. Hawkins, and B. N. Uchino. "Hostility, anger, and marital adjustment: concurrent and prospective associations with psychosocial vulnerability." *Journal of Behavioral Medicine* 30 (2007): 1–10.

Baron-Cohen, Simon. *The Essential Difference: Male and Female Brains and the Truth about Autism.* New York: Basic Books, 2004.

Baruch, Grace, and Rosalind Barnett. "Adult daughters' relationships with their mothers: the era of good feelings." *Journal of Marriage and the Family* 45, no. 3 (1983): 601–6.

Bateson, Gregory. *Steps to an Ecology of Mind.* New York: Ballantine, 1972.

Bloom, Amy. "Dead, thank God." In *I Married My Mother-in-Law: And Other Tales of In-Laws We Can't Live With—and Can't Live Without.* Edited by Ilena Silverman. New York: Riverhead, 2007.

Brooks-Gunn, Jean, and Frank Furstenberg. "Long-term implications of fertility-related behavior and family formation on adolescent mothers and their children." In *Family Systems and Life-Span Development.* Edited by Kurt Kreppner and Richard M. Lerner. Hillsdale, NJ: Lawrence Erlbaum Associates, 1989, pp. 319–39.

Burger, J. M., and R. M. Huntzinger. "Temporal effects on attribution for one's own behavior: the role of task outcome." *Journal of Experimental Social Psychology* 21 (1985): 247–61. http://scholar.google.co.uk/scholar?hl=en&lr=&client=firefox-a&cluster=13470837868046007850.

Byng-Hall, J. "Symptom-bearer as marital distance regulator." *Family Process* 19 (1980): 355–65.

CarersUK. http://www.carersuk.org.

CarersUK. *Without us . . . ? Calculating the value of carers' support.* London: CarersUK, 2002.

Catan, Liza. Youth, Citizenship and Social Change. Economic & Social Research Council, 2002.

Chabon, Michael. "My father-in-law, briefly." In *I Married My Mother-in-Law: And Other Tales of In-Laws We Can't Live With—and Can't Live Without.* Edited by Ilena Silverman. New York: Riverhead, 2007.

Cocola, Nancy Wasserman. *Six in the Bed: Dealing with Parents, In-Laws and Their Impact on Your Marriage.* New York: Perigee, 1997.

Dicks, Henry. *Marital Tensions.* London: Routledge, 1967.

di Giovanni, Janine. "Mothers-in-law who are no joke." *The Telegraph* (London; December 7, 2007).

Dunn, Judy. *Family Relationships: Children's Perspectives.* London: One Plus One, 2008.

Dunn, Judy, and Robert Plomin. *Separate Lives: Why Siblings Are So Different.* New York: Basic Books, 1992.

Duras, Marguerite. "The stolen pigeons." Translated from the French by Deborah Treisman. *The New Yorker* (April 16, 2007): 138–49.

Duvall, Evelyn Ruth. *In-Laws, Pro and Con: An Original Study of Interpersonal Relations*. New York: Hill & Wang, 1954.

Dweck, Carol. *Mindset: The New Psychology of Success*. New York: Random House, 2006.

EU.R.E.S. "Un divorzio ogni quattro minuti." Rome: Ricerche Economiche e Sociali, November 9, 2006. http://www.eures.it/upload/1224677799.pdf.

Eaker, E. D., L. M. Sullivan, M. Kelly-Hayes, R. B. D'Agostino, Sr., and E. J. Benjamin. "Marital status, marital strain and the risk of coronary heart disease or total mortality: the Framingham offspring study." *Psychosomatic Medicine* 69 (2007): 509–13.

Fearnley-Wittingstall, Jane. *The Good Granny Guide: Or How to Be a Modern Grandmother*. London: Short Books, 2006.

Fine, Cordelia. *A Mind of Its Own: How the Brain Distorts and Deceives*. New York: W. W. Norton, 2007.

Fischer, Lucy Rose. "Mothers and mothers-in-law." *Journal of Marriage and the Family* (February 1983): 187–92.

Fishel, Elizabeth. *Sisters: Shared Histories, Lifelong Ties*. Red Wheel/Weiser, 1997.

Forshaw, Mark J. "Free qualitative research from the shackles of method." *The Psychologist* 20, no. 8 (August 2007): 478–79.

Fortes, Meyer, ed. *Marriage in Tribal Societies*. Cambridge: Cambridge University Press, 1962.

———. *Rules and the Emergence of Society*. London: Royal Anthropological Institute, 1983.

———. *The Web of Kinship among the Tallensi*. Oxford, UK: Oxford University Press, 1949.

Frean, Alexandra. "No joke for mother-in-law." *The Times* (London; December 21, 1999): 1.

Gallin, Rita S. "The intersection of class and age: mother-in-law and daughter-in-law relations in rural Taiwan." *Journal of Cross-Cultural Gerontology* 9, no. 2 (April 1994): 127–40.

Gates, Henry Louis. "Hating Hillary." *The New Yorker* (February 26, 1996).

George, Mike. *It could be you: A report on the chances of becoming a carer*. London: CarersUK, 2001.

Gladwell, Malcolm. *Blink: The Power of Thinking Without Thinking*. Boston: Little, Brown and Co., 2005.

Globerman, Judith. "Motivations to care: daughters- and sons-in-law caring for relatives with Alzheimer's disease." *Family Relations* 45 (1996): 37–45.

Goody, Jack. *The Development of the Family and Marriage in Europe.* Cambridge, UK: Cambridge University Press, 1983.

————, ed. *Kinship: Selected Readings.* Penguin Modern Sociology Readings. London: Penguin, 1971.

————. "The labyrinth of kinship." *New Left Review* 36 (November–December 2005).

Goody, Jack, and S. J. Tambiah. *Bridewealth and Dowry.* Cambridge, UK: Cambridge University Press, 1973.

Gottman, John, with Nan Silver. *Why Marriages Succeed or Fail.* New York: Fireside, 1994.

Grandparents Association. http://www.grandparents-association.org.uk.

Grandparents Plus. http://www.grandparentsplus.org.uk/information/statistics.html.

Gross, Jane. "Elder-care costs deplete savings of a generation." *New York Times* (December 30, 2006).

Hagestad, Gunhild. "Parent-child relations in later life: trends and gaps in past research." In *Parenting Across the Lifespan: Biosocial Dimensions.* Edited by Jane Lancaster, Jeanne Altmann, Alice Rossi, and Lonnite Sherrod. New York: Aldine de Gruyter, 1987, pp. 405–33.

Hawkes, K. "The grandmother effect." *Nature* 428 (2004): 128–29.

Hitchcock, Amanda. "Rising number of dowry deaths in India." World Socialist Web Site, July 4, 2001. http://www.wsws.org/articles/2001/jul2001/ind-j04.shtml.

Hobbs, Frank, and Nicole Stoops. U.S. Census Bureau, Census 2000 Special Reports, Series CENSR-4, *Demographic Trends in the 20th Century.* Washington, D.C.: U.S. Government Printing Office, 2002.

Hochschild, Arlie Russel, with Anne Machung. *The Second Shift.* New York: Viking, 1989.

Horsley, Gloria Call. *In-Laws: A Guide to Extended Family Therapy.* New York: J. Wiley and Sons, 1995.

————. *The In-Law Survival Manual: A Guide to Cultivating Healthy In-Law Relationships.* New York: Chichester, Wiley, 1997.

Instituto Nazionale di Statistica. "Matrimoni, separazioni e divorzi: anno 2003." Rome: Istat, 2006.

Irwin, Aisling. "Mother-in-law can't help spoiling a wife's Christmas." *The Telegraph* (London; December 21, 1999): 1.

Jack, Dana Crowley. *Silencing the Self: Women and Depression.* Cambridge, MA: Harvard University Press, 1991.

Jensen, Robert, and Emily Oster. *The Power of TV: Cable Television Raises Women's Status in India.* NBER Working Paper no. 13305. National Bureau of Economic Research (August 2007).

Kirkpatrick, Clifford. *The Family as Process and Institution.* 2nd ed. New York: Roland Press, 1963, pp. 470–71.

Knight, Will. "Elderly crucial to evolutionary success of human." *New Scientist* 6 (July 2004).

MacMahon, Barbara. "Mama's boys fuel Italy's soaring divorce rate." *The Observer* (November 12, 2006).

McPhee, Martha. "Longing for in-laws." In *I Married My Mother-in-Law: And Other Tales of In-Laws We Can't Live With—and Can't Live Without.* Edited by Ilena Silverman. New York: Riverhead, 2007.

Mooney, A., J. Statham, and A. Simon. *The pivot generation: Informal care and work after fifty.* Thomas Coram Research Unit, Institute of Education, University of London. Commissioned by the Joseph Rowntree Fund. Bristol, UK: The Policy Press, 2002.

Nealey-Moore, J. B., T. W. Smith, B. N. Uchino, M. W. Hawkins, and C. Olson-Cerny. "Cardiovascular reactivity during positive and negative marital interactions." *Journal of Behavioral Medicine* (2007).

Norton, Arthur, and Louisa Miller. U.S. Bureau of the Census, Current Population Reports, P23-180, *Marriage, Divorce, and Remarriage in the 1990's.* Washington, D.C.: U.S. Government Printing Office, 1992.

O'Connell, Martin, and Gretchen Gooding. *Comparison of ACS and ASEC Data on Households and Families: 2004.* Population Division, U.S. Census Bureau. http://www.census.gov/acs/www/Downloads/ACS.ASEC.Comp.Report.Apr11.doc.

Office for National Statistics. *Social Trends.* 38th ed. New York: Palgrave Macmillan, 2008.

Parker-Pope, Tara. "Marital spats, taken to heart." *New York Times* (October 2, 2007).

Patterson, Gerald, and Marion Forgatch. *Parents and Adolescents Living Together: Part 1, The Basics.* Vol. 1, 2nd ed. Champaign, IL: Research Press, 2005.

Phillips, Estelle. "On becoming a mother-in-law." *The New Psychologist* 9 (1995): 65–72.

Pinker, Steven. *How the Mind Works.* New York: W. W. Norton, 1999.

Radcliffe-Brown, A. R., and Daryll Forde, eds. *African Systems of Kinship and Marriage.* London: International African Institute, 1987.

Richmond, Peter. "I married my mother-in-law." In *I Married My Mother-in-*

Law: And Other Tales of In-Laws We Can't Live With—and Can't Live Without. Edited by Ilena Silverman. New York: Riverhead, 2007.

Seligman, Martin. Learned Optimism. 2nd ed. New York: Pocket Books (Simon and Schuster), 1998.

Seligson, Hannah. A Little Bit Married. New York: DaCapo Books, 2009.

Shapiro, Dani. "My mother's four rules of family life." In I Married My Mother-in-Law: And Other Tales of In-Laws We Can't Live With—and Can't Live Without. Edited by Ilena Silverman. New York: Riverhead, 2007.

Skynner, Robin. One Flesh: Separate Person. London: Constable, 1976.

Skynner, Robin, and John Cleese. Families and How to Survive Them. London: Methuen, 1983.

Smith, T. W., and K. Glazer. "Hostility, marriage, and the heart: The social psychophysiology of cardiovascular risk in close relationships." In Handbook of Families and Health: Interdisciplinary Perspectives. Edited by D. R. Crane and E. S. Marshall. Thousand Oaks, CA: Sage Publications, 2006, pp. 19–39.

Straight, Susan. "In-laws you can't divorce." In I Married My Mother-in-Law: And Other Tales of In-Laws We Can't Live With—and Can't Live Without. Edited by Ilena Silverman. New York: Riverhead, 2007.

Sweet, James A., and Larry L. Bumpass. National Survey of Families and Households, Waves 1 and 2: Data Description and Documentation. Center for Demography and Ecology, University of Wisconsin–Madison. http://www.ssc.wisc.edu/nsfh/home.htm.

Taggart, Michael. "Will your bathroom pass the test?" Daily Mail (August 31, 2004).

Tannen, Deborah. You Just Don't Understand: Women and Men in Conversation. New York: Morrow, 1990.

U.S. Bureau of the Census. Families and Living Arrangements, Current Population Survey Report, 2005 March CPS. Table A1. Marital Status of People 15 Years and Over, by Age, Sex, Personal Earnings, Race, and Hispanic Origin: 2005. http://www.census.gov/population/www/socdemo/hh-fam/cps2005.html.

U.S. Bureau of the Census. Families and Living Arrangements, Current Population Survey Report, 2006 March CPS. Table A1. Marital Status of People 15 Years and Over, by Age, Sex, Personal Earnings, Race, and Hispanic Origin: 2006. http://www.census.gov/population/www/socdemo/hh-fam/cps2006.html.

U.S. Bureau of the Census. Families and Living Arrangements, Historical Time

Series, Marital status. Table MS-1: Marital Status of the Population 15 Years Old and Over, by Sex and Race: 1950 to Present. http://www.census.gov/population/www/socdemo/hh-fam.html#ht.

U.S. Bureau of the Census. Grandparents and Grandchildren. http://www.census.gov/population/www/socdemo/grandparents.html.

U.S. Bureau of the Census. Marriage and Divorce. The U.S. Census Bureau does not collect the number of marriages and divorces that take place in a given year. http://www.census.gov/population/www/socdemo/marr-div.html.

U.S. Bureau of Statistics. Families and Living Arrangements. http://www.census.gov/population/www/socdemo/hh-fam.html.

Viorst, Judith. *Necessary Losses: The Loves, Illusions, Dependencies, and Impossible Expectations That All of Us Have to Give Up in Order to Grow*. New York: Simon and Schuster, 1986.

Waldman, Ayelet. "Dividing a man from his mother." In *I Married My Mother-in-Law: And Other Tales of In-Laws We Can't Live With—and Can't Live Without*. Edited by Ilena Silverman. New York: Riverhead, 2007.

Walton, G. M., and G. L. Cohen. "Stereotype lift." *Journal of Experimental Social Psychology* 39 (2003): 456–67.

Wedekind, C., Seebeck, T., Bettens, F., and Paepke, A. J. "MHC-dependent mate preferences in humans." *Proceedings of the Royal Society* 260 (1995): 245–49.

Winston, Robert. *The Human Mind: And How to Make the Most of It*. New York: Transworld Publishers, 2004.

Young, Michael, and Gerard Lemos. "Family and kinship revisited." *Prospect Magazine* 27 (February 1998).

Youniss, James, and Jacqueline Smollar. *Adolescent Relations with Mothers, Fathers and Friends*. Chicago, IL: University of Chicago Press, 1985.

Index